The Measure of a Christian

Living for a Legacy in Christ

Tim May

Sermon To Book
www.sermontobook.com

The Measure of a Christian / Tim May
ISBN-13: 978-1-945793-43-1
ISBN-10: 1-945793-43-0

To Matthew, Melody, and Aniya—

Three amazing children who inspire me to live a legacy that matters!

CONTENTS

Acknowledgments

Greetings! It is difficult to imagine yourself a preacher if you have no one to hear the sermon. Therefore, I am genuinely grateful for the men, women, boys, and girls of First United Methodist Church of Fort Pierce, Florida. These friends not only listened to my sermons, but they also showed me what a legacy in Christ might look like.

I have been involved with the military all of my life. The military is where I learned such terms as *honor*, *legacy*, and *commitment*. I am forever indebted to the sacrifices that these men and women and their families have made for the cause of peace and freedom. It has been a real honor and privilege to serve as a Navy chaplain to these patriots.

Finally, I want to thank my beautiful wife, Jackie. She has been by my side since I first learned how to write a sermon. If people were to earn a seat at God's table for having endured poorly written and preached sermons, she would most certainly receive a place at the head of the table because of my many terrible attempts she has had to weather. She is my number one encourager. But more than that, she is my true partner in helping me create a legacy in Christ. Thank you, Jackie, for believing in me and for continually reminding me that I have what it takes to be a pastor of God's people!

INTRODUCTION

Three Key Questions

The lamp of the body is the eye. If therefore your eye is good, your whole body will be full of light. But if your eye is bad, your whole body will be full of darkness. If therefore the light that is in you is darkness, how great is that darkness!
— Matthew 6:22–23 (NKJV)

When life gets messy, how do you respond? Some Christians seem to shine God's light even brighter during times of trial or suffering. For others, our lights become much dimmer as we struggle through hard times.

It's a simple question, and yet in many ways, it's the foundation of our life in Christ.

A few years ago, I ran a 5K. The next day I experienced a bit of pain. I thought I had tweaked my back or pulled a muscle on the run, so I went on with my normal routine, figuring the discomfort would ease as the day progressed. But as time went on, I knew something wasn't right. The pain was getting worse.

I scheduled an appointment with my doctor for the

following day. By the time I arrived at his office, the pain had increased to the point that I couldn't even get up onto the examining table. I was doubled over, could barely walk, and I feared the worst.

The doctor took one look at me and told me I needed to go to the emergency room. (In retrospect, I probably should have done that to begin with!)

Once I arrived at the ER, the doctors immediately put me on a gurney and rushed me in for an emergency appendectomy.

Panicked thoughts swarmed my mind, as the stress of the situation sank in. I had done nothing to prepare for this—I was completely caught off guard. Furthermore, my family had no idea where I was or that I was about to undergo surgery. I was completely helpless in a high-stress situation.

I could have panicked and fought the idea of surgery every step of the way. I could have begged the doctors to wait another day or two, allowing me to be more ready for what was to come. I could have even demanded a second opinion or made it difficult for them to prep me for surgery.

But every moment spent fighting this life-saving procedure would only cause me more pain, more suffering, and more hardship.

Yes, I was going into surgery alone. Yes, I was terrified, frustrated, and even a bit angry. But I knew that by accepting what was happening and acknowledging it was for my own good, I was allowing the doctors and nurses to do what they do best: save my life.

How we react in moments of stress, frustration, hardship, or challenge does a lot to determine whether the situation will get better or worse.

In fact, how we react when life spirals out of our control is a measure of our Christianity.

Blind Spots

In the folktale "The Emperor's New Clothes" by Hans Christian Andersen, two weavers convince an emperor obsessed with fine clothing to commission them to weave a special set of clothes. According to the weavers, anyone who was unwise or unsuitable for his or her job would think these new clothes were invisible.

Of course, the vain emperor found this prospect very exciting and paid the dishonest weavers' exorbitant fees. Meanwhile, the court advisors played along, pretending the clothes were beautiful, because they didn't want the emperor to think they were foolish or unqualified. And the emperor himself played along, even though he, too, failed to see his new suit of clothes—not realizing the weavers were con artists and the clothes were nonexistent, not merely invisible.

In fact, the emperor decided to hold a parade to show off his new wardrobe, and his subjects played along, fawning over the new clothes they couldn't see.

Except, that is, for one child in the crowd, who innocently remarked that the emperor was wearing no clothing at all.

I can only imagine how embarrassed and angry the emperor must have felt. He'd been so confident in the new clothes that he failed to realize they weren't there at all.

What happened to the king is what happens to us when we walk through life unaware of our blind spots. When we aren't striving to become more Christlike, then our blind spots can take over, making it that much easier to slide back into old sin.

King David had a blind spot. Scripture says it was time to go to war, but David chose to stay home. His blind spot caused him to believe he was above fighting in the battle.

While enjoying life at home, David noticed a woman across the way taking a bath and decided he wanted to have her for himself.

He brought Bathsheba into his home and ended up having a sexual encounter with her resulting in a pregnancy. Again, David's blind spots continued to cloud his vision. He brought Bathsheba's husband, Uriah, home from the war, thinking he could convince Uriah to sleep with his wife. Uriah would think he was the father and no one would find out about David's sin.

Unfortunately for David (as far as resolving his personal situation), Uriah was a devoted soldier who steadfastly abstained from sleeping with his wife during wartime. He told David no: "Shall I then go to my house to eat and drink, and to lie with my wife? As you live, and as your soul lives, I will not do this thing" (2 Samuel 11:11 NKJV). David's blind spot prevented him from appreciating Uriah's dedication to the kingdom.

David decided to get Uriah drunk. Maybe while he was drunk, he would sleep with his wife. But again, Uriah would not dishonor his fellow soldiers and the head of the army, King David. Finally, David wrote out and sent an order with Uriah to Joab, his general. The order told Joab to attack the enemy, but specifically, to make sure Uriah was in the front of the battle procession. When the battle grew heaviest, David commanded Joab to retreat and leave Uriah exposed. Joab withdrew the troops just as David had ordered, leaving Uriah exposed.

David's blind spots were revealed, but no one would confront him; no one would tell the king he was not wearing any clothes.

When we are not aware of our blind spots, all kinds of things can happen. When we are not aware of our blind spots, we often spend time and energy trying to put forth a certain image of who we are. We try to act a certain way and sound a certain way even if it doesn't truly re-flect our inner selves.

Discovering your blind spots will take work, but you will waste energy and time trying to hide who you really are if you choose to ignore them. If you continue to go through life believing you don't have any blind spots, you will likely end up causing destruction along the way. You may begin relationships, say things to people, or do things you ought not to do because of these blind spots.

Fortunately, although King David sinned with Bath-sheba, he begged God in Psalm 139 to reveal the issues in his heart that were not pleasing:

> *Search me, O God, and know my heart; try me, and know my anxieties; and see if there is any wicked way in me, and lead me in the way everlasting.*
> *— Psalm 139:23–24 (NKJV)*

King David asked God to show him his blind spots. Followers of Jesus should do the same—and should be willing to accept what God reveals.

I confess I sometimes want God to reveal my blind spots, to reveal the things keeping me from being all He intended for me to be and from leading others well, but I want Him to do it in little bitty steps. I want the pain to come in small doses. This, too, reveals a blind spot: it communicates that I am not sure I can trust God's love. I am not sure I can trust God with His revelation.

If we trust God to reveal blind spots, knowing He does so out of love, then we can feel comfortable in inviting Him to reveal those blind spots as we pray and read the Bible. Our first steps should be to approach Him in prayer and to read the Bible. Rather than coming up with our own conclusions about what we think our blind spots are, we can allow the Holy Spirit and the Word to illuminate things that might be preventing us from being useful servants of God.

An additional step may be to invite "Nathans" into our lives. Nathan was the prophet who came alongside David and pointed out what his issue was (2 Samuel 12). Nathan was a trusted friend because he loved God and followed God's teachings. His integrity with God secured him the access to speak to the king.

Our blind spots can lead us to surround ourselves with people who are afraid to tell us hard truths, as if we were the emperor who thought he was wearing fine new clothes. By inviting a trusted friend who loves God and His Word to point out when you, like the emperor, are living by a deception or falsehood, you can get closer to finding and fixing your blind spots.

Facing the Truth

Embarrassment and anger are powerful emotions. Most of us have a hard time hiding them when they pop up—and that means they can quickly affect the way we respond to life situations.

Nothing tends to spark embarrassment or anger more than having someone point out something unpleasant that we weren't previously aware of. Like the poor soul walking down the street with no clothes, our knee-jerk reaction is usually one of embarrassment, and we often cover that embarrassment by lashing out in anger.

Having our mistakes or errors pointed out is not necessarily a bad thing. But our reaction to those critiques matters.

Perhaps you have experienced a monthly review at work where your performance was evaluated, and you were given feedback on areas of improvement.

There are not many people I know who find that to be an enjoyable experience. Still, the process is important because, if you are working for a fair-minded boss, he will give you an honest assessment you can use to improve your job performance and ultimately (hopefully) increase your paycheck.

What if you were to become angry at him for his assessment? Or what if you were to take what he told you and ignore it? Or what if your boss knew you to be an easily aggravated person, and so he withheld the truth from you, only to fire you later?

How we react to being told about our blind spots—the flaws other people see but we don't—is another measure of our Christianity.

If we don't welcome the criticism of others, and if we are not willing to go through the process of discovering our blind spots, we will be much like the emperor going out on parade with no clothes on.

Or we'll be the employee who never improves, is difficult to approach, and ends up being passed up for promotions and opportunities.

Bottom line: by our lack of humility and unwillingness to learn, we won't be reflecting Christ.

Expecting the Worst

Suppose you go to the doctor for your annual checkup, and the doctor tells you that you need to go on a diet and start taking medication for high blood pressure. You might respond one of two ways.

You might leave his office believing he's full of nonsense and he's just trying to earn a kickback from the drug company.

Alternatively, you might accept his diagnosis, realize you have a problem, and gratefully follow the doctor's recommendations, recognizing he is trying to help you improve your life.

Or what about the mechanic who comes to you with a list of things that need to be fixed—and all you wanted was an oil change!

You could jump to conclusions and assume he is trying to swindle you out of time and money. Or you could thank him for his assessment and either make a plan to get those repairs taken care of or ask for some time to think about it.

How we respond in day-to-day situations—not just the big stuff, but the little stuff, too—says a lot about who we are in Christ.

Character Revealed

When life spirals out of control, when someone points out our blind spots, when the day-to-day gets to us— these are three areas in which it's easy to let negativity and anger take hold.

How do you react when your boss gives you news you don't like? What goes through your mind when your doctor gives you a diagnosis you're not happy with? What's your response when the mechanic tells you the repairs on your car are going to cost more than you thought?

The way we react to difficult situations reveals our true character. It also reveals our relationship with Christ.

Stressful or distressing situations are a test as to what's going on inside our hearts and minds. We can respond with cynicism, doubt, and fear. Or we can respond from a place of confidence as we draw on strength from within.

When a Marine recruit has reached the end of his or her training, that individual is generally sent out on a "crucible" event—a forty-eight-hour period during which the recruit is only allowed to eat two meals. That individual is also required to hike close to twenty-eight miles and is given a multitude of obligatory exercises.

A crucible is a ceramic container that allows substances to be heated to extremely high temperatures and removes all impurities. This test is called the crucible because it's meant to test that person's mettle under extreme circumstances and acts as the final step in the creation of a true Marine.

On the West Coast, the recruits are required to climb a mountain called the "Widow Maker"—a name that indicates just how tough it is. By the time a recruit reaches the Widow Maker, he or she has already been through eight weeks of rigorous training and has not had proper rest or eaten much. At this point, recruits are likely at the end of their rope, fighting the desire to throw in the towel and go home.

Yet these hopefuls somehow must find the strength to keep going.

It is at that point—when they are at their lowest physically, emotionally, and mentally—their true character as a Marine is revealed.

Those who make it through are rewarded with their Eagle, Globe, and Anchor, but even more importantly, they receive the title of Marine.

In much the same way, when people are put to the test, their crucible events provide opportunities to show their mettle and earn the title worth striving for—Christian.

It was when Jesus hung on the cross after being mocked, beaten, and humiliated—in horrible pain—that the true character of God was revealed in Him.

When Jesus said, "Father, forgive them; for they know not what they do" (Luke 23:34 KJV), God's unconditional love and forgiveness was revealed.

His desire for His children to know they matter and He will never stop loving them, whatever happens, was clear. He went to extreme lengths to prove this to us. Jesus never lost focus.

Finding Light in the Darkness

In Matthew 6:22–23, Jesus said that if a person's eyes—their vision—is *healthy*, their body will be full of light. But, if their vision is *unhealthy*, they will be filled with darkness.

Was Jesus talking about actual eyesight? No. Rather, He was talking about focus.

If a person's focus remains on Him, and if they are abiding in Him, they will have His light and His strength within them—the source of their strength in trials of every kind.

However, if their vision is cloudy and their focus is not on Jesus, then they are not abiding in Him. Their character will be infected with darkness that will be revealed to others by how they react and respond to difficult situations.

No matter how we try to hide it, if we are not abiding in Jesus, if we are not connected to Him through the Holy Spirit, we will fall short of the finish line during crucible events. Our darkness will be revealed, and we won't make it up that mountain.

How can we discern whether or not we rely on God's

strength when going through a trial? Here are three key questions:

1. When faced with difficulties, do you move toward God or away from God? The prophet Elijah had a wonderful experience on Mount Carmel. He had taken on the prophets of Baal and emerged victorious.

That alone was an amazing feat and one might think was the pinnacle of Elijah's crucible event. But then another trial came against him; the queen at the time put a bounty on Elijah's head. People were hunting him.

Elijah reacted in a less-than-honorable way and, instead of facing the situation, ran off and hid in a cave. It was so bad that God met him in that cave and asked him why he had run away—why was he hiding?

Like many of us, Elijah had performed admirably during the first part of the test, but he fell short in the second part. His faith was only strong enough for one trial, not a series of trials. When things stayed difficult, Elijah stopped trusting in God's protection and provision.

Elijah moved away from God instead of toward Him.

Job also faced a crucible event—actually, a series of them. Life was great for Job. He had a good job, lots of money, a nice house, and a great family. Then he lost everything. He lost his business, his family, and his money. On top of all that, he became infected with a string of terrible diseases; the Bible says he suffered from boils upon boils.

How did Job react to all this? Though he expressed plenty of emotion and frustration, he remained close to God. He refused to turn inward.

Job moved toward God, not away from Him.

What about you? Do you run and hide when troubles come your way, or do you move closer to God?

2. Do you trust God to provide a solution? Whatever problems or challenges you face, do you trust God will bring you out of it? Do you trust He will make a way through them when there appears to be a dead end?

At one point during their forty-year trek through the desert, the Israelites were starving to death. There was no food for as far as the eye could see. In fact, they had become so desperate they thought it would be better to go back to Egypt where they had been enslaved and mistreated, because at least there they had food.

Though they couldn't see a way out, God provided a solution. Where there was no food, God created food. He sent them manna from heaven.

In the moment of provision, they were quick to celebrate and praise God for His goodness and faithfulness. However, as soon as they came across another hurdle, they would revert to panic and doubt. Their complaining reflected a lack of trust that God would continue to provide.

It's easy to shake our heads at the Israelites' lack of trust, but we should consider whether we do the same thing in our own lives.

Has there been a time when you were faced with a problem and you panicked, swept away by anxiety or fear? Has there been a time when God provided a solution, and you were happy and renewed in your spirit—until another problem came along and you panicked again?

God's children notoriously have short memories. We either forget how God has provided for us previously, or we believe that, for whatever reason, He won't do it again.

There are also times we simply don't like the solution God provides. Just like the Israelites, we don't necessarily *like* manna from heaven and would prefer steak and potatoes. God has offered a solution, but we believe we have a better one. Sometimes we may even cry out, "Is there another god out there? Because this one is not listening to the solution I believe He should provide!"

When I visited California years ago for a business I was launching, in my mind I already had a clear picture in my mind of what I anticipated God would do.

I *expected* He would put His blessing on my new business and make it successful. I believed I was stepping out in faith by starting that business, and I had the solution already laid out in my mind.

But God said, "I have another solution for you. Here is what you are going to do. You're going to be recalled into active duty, and you're going to short-sell your house. On top of that, you're going to have a baby."

"God," I said, "I don't like that solution. Can I have another, more in line with what I had planned?" I dug my heels into the ground and would not acknowledge God's solution was better than mine—which leads to the third question:

3. Do you surrender to the solutions God provides?
Surrender is not easy. It means submitting your will to

another.

In Western society, the word *surrender* carries negative connotations, and many associate it with weakness. But with God, surrender is the opposite. It is a sign of strength.

The Bible says, "No one can serve two masters, for either he will hate the one and love the other, or he will be devoted to the one and despise the other" (Matthew 6:24).

We cannot be in control and at the same time surrender control to God. We cannot follow our own solution and at the same time allow God to provide the solution.

To truly rely on God, to truly lean on His strength, we must completely surrender to the solutions God provides. We must choose to work with them—even if they're solutions we don't necessarily like.

The Israelites failed to surrender to God's solution completely. When God sent manna from heaven, He told them to eat until they had their fill and then to leave the rest. They were not to save manna for the next day; more would be provided when they needed it.

However, the people didn't entirely trust this plan; after they had eaten their fill, some went and collected extra to have for the next day. The problem was that by the next day the manna was putrid and inedible.

The Israelites trusted God a little bit, but not completely. They figured they'd hedge their bets a little by holding on to a few extra pieces of manna, just in case. They didn't fully surrender to God's solution, and eventually, they realized their solution didn't work.

When we find ourselves in an overwhelming situation

that seems hopeless, we must trust that the solution God provides is working toward our good.

God sees beyond our current circumstances, and when He provides a solution, it is with the whole picture of our lives in mind. Even if the solution presented to us doesn't seem like our ideal, we must trust that God knows what He is doing as we fully surrender to His plan.

Feeding the Right Wolf

When I was called back on active duty, I followed God's solution for my life and spent three years working in the substance abuse recovery program with the Navy. During that time, I came across a Cherokee Indian story that reminds us what we feed our souls will have power in our lives.

A little boy and his grandfather sat by the fire. The boy was visibly upset and angry over something that did not go his way. After a time, the grandfather said to his grandson, "A fight is going on inside of me. It is a terrible fight between two wolves. One is evil—he is anger, envy, sorrow, regret, greed, arrogance, self-pity, guilt, resentment, inferiority, lies, false pride, superiority, and ego." He continued, "The other is good—he is joy, peace, love, hope, serenity, humility, kindness, benevolence, empathy, generosity, truth, compassion, and faith. The same fight is going on inside you—and inside every other person, too."

The grandson thought about it for a minute and then asked his grandfather, "Which wolf will win?" The grandfather simply replied, "The one you feed."

Christians face that same choice every day. Surrendering to God's solution is the only real way to discover God's strength within—it's the only way to discover what it is you are feeding.

- Are you feeding fear by not inviting people into your life who will lovingly point out the blind spots?
- Are you feeding control by trying to modify God's solution to fit more neatly with your own?
- Are you feeding worry by placing your concerns into God's hands but then taking them back so you can fret over them?
- Are you feeding anger at not having things go exactly your way?

Feeding these negative emotions takes focus and energy away from living according to God's strength as "more than a conqueror" (Romans 8:37). Left unfed, our trust and dependence will eventually become disconnected from God and die—and a life disconnected from God is a life left unfulfilled.

The pathway to discovering God's strength within is a pathway to freedom. It involves moving toward God. It involves trusting that God has a solution. And finally, it requires fully surrendering to God's plan.

Every test and trial is an opportunity to develop character as a Christian and to grow in faith. It's in difficult times that character is not only revealed but is shaped and developed.

To help you with this, we've provided a workbook section after each chapter. This workbook includes reflection questions for you to consider as well as steps to take to apply the content of each chapter to your life. Each chapter ends with a page for taking any notes that you might like.

No one likes troubles and challenges, but without those crucible events, you might miss the chance to test your mettle and earn the title of "Christian." These events allow you to find your measure, and if you let them, they will shape your life so that you can leave behind a legacy of following Christ's example.

CHAPTER ONE

Hedging Your Bets

*"Now therefore," he said, "put away the foreign gods
which are among you, and incline your heart to the LORD
God of Israel."*

— *Joshua 24:23 (NKJV)*

Once when I was stationed with the Marines as a battalion chaplain, my unit was sent to Clear Creek, Idaho,
to fight fires in the Salmon-Challis National Forest. We
camped in the middle of a cow pasture, just over the
mountain range from where the fires were burning. We
would traverse the mountain every day to fight the fires
and return to our campsite in the evening.

It was an actual cow pasture, with cattle grazing
around us. There was no electricity, so there were no tel-
evisions and no computers—basically, nothing to keep a
bunch of Marines occupied. The average age was between seventeen and nineteen, so they tended to grow a
little bored. To curb their boredom, they came up with
creative ways to occupy themselves.

One Marine found a caterpillar out on the grass and brought it to one of his buddies. "I bet you won't swallow this caterpillar," he said. His buddy asked him how much he'd be willing to put up on the bet, and the Marine with the caterpillar put up a whopping five dollars. His buddy took the bet and shoved the caterpillar in his mouth.

About a minute and a half later, the Marine had to be seen by emergency responders because the caterpillar bit the inside of the guy's throat. His throat began to swell to the point where he couldn't breathe, but it was too late to pull the caterpillar out. He was all in, like it or not. This big, tough Marine had yielded himself to a caterpillar for five dollars, and he put himself in mortal jeopardy because of it.

Of course, that story is a negative example of being "all in," but consider another situation. Todd Beamer was a passenger on Flight 93 on 9/11. He was the passenger who said, "Are you ready? Okay. Let's roll."

Beamer went all in with his fellow passengers to stop the terrorists on Flight 93 as it flew toward its intended target in Washington, D.C. Because of Todd Beamer, fellow passengers, and crew members, the plane crashed prematurely in a field near Shanksville, Somerset County, Pennsylvania. Everyone on board was killed, but those brave people saved countless others at the plane's intended target.

When Todd Beamer said, "Let's roll," he declared that he and the others were all in. Nothing was going to hold them back, and they were prepared to do whatever it took to stop the hijackers from reaching their target.

They yielded themselves wholeheartedly to the mission, with unwavering conviction.

Going All In

In the Bible, Joshua speaks to the Israelites as they are about to enter the Promised Land (Joshua 24). He tells them of the need to follow God wholeheartedly or not at all.

Many people who declare themselves Christ-followers will often have the best intentions, but when it comes down to it, they won't follow through. They lack the conviction Joshua was talking about when he said to his people, "Incline your heart to the LORD God of Israel" (Joshua 24:23 NKJV).

He was talking about being "all in," wherever the consequences led.

Being a "good Christian" is measured by the posture of your heart and your willingness to yield to God at any cost. Many Christians might be willing to take the risk and give it a try, but might not be willing to go all in. When they yield their hearts to God, they hold back just a bit to minimize the risk just in case things don't go as planned. In other words, they like to play it safe when it comes to living the Christian life.

Playing It Safe

When I was stationed with the Marines in California, I attended several Marine Corps functions, which for some reason always took place in or near Las Vegas,

Nevada—a place with many an opportunity for betting and gambling.

I was the kind of person who tends to play it safe when it comes to betting. I didn't really understand the rules of the card games, the roulette wheels, and other complex games of chance. At the time, I tended toward the "one-armed bandits," better known as the slot machines. They made sense to me.

This was back in the day when slot machines only accepted coins. I'd cash in twenty-five dollars and put my twenty-five dollars' worth of coins in a cup. Then I'd grab a second cup that I intended to fill with my winnings.

My plan was to keep my winnings separate, and as I began to win, I would play with the extra money in the "winnings" cup. This way, I would play with the "house money," and in the end, I would still have my original twenty-five dollars. It was basically risk-free gambling. I could put my original twenty-five bucks back in my pocket and at least break even in the end.

Christians sometimes do the same, playing life with house money. Rather than being all in, they hold back a little, just in case. But God is asking us to bet on Him—to go all in, realizing that *He went all in for us.*

All throughout the Scriptures, God gave His all to ensure that we would be saved and united with Him. He has been using His created people from the beginning to fulfill His plan of redemption—ultimately giving up His life so that we could have life abundant (John 10:10).

When we think about this abundant life, it's easy to associate it with a comfortable lifestyle. In fact, Jesus taught that the opposite was true.

The Bible tells a story of a rich young man who came to Jesus and asked what he must do to inherit eternal life. Jesus told him that he should follow the commandments. The young man replied that he had done so since his youth. So Jesus took the conversation one step further and told him that he must go and sell all his possessions, give the money to the poor, and then come and follow Him.

When the man heard this, he became disheartened because he was quite wealthy; the price of eternal life must have seemed a little too steep (Luke 18:18–23). Jesus wanted that man to bet on God, and to be all in. However, the young man was not quite ready to give everything up and take the bet.

Many people think this story means we must sell everything we have and give the money to the poor. However, there is a much deeper meaning: Jesus doesn't want us to play it safe by holding back—He wants us to be fully committed to Him with everything that is in us.

For some, this might mean giving up our worldly goods. "Everything," however, is more than material possessions. Giving up everything to follow Jesus means giving your hopes, your dreams, your ambitions, and your future projections to God.

It means surrendering the fullness of your life, knowing He gave the fullness of His life for you.

Right here, right now, God is inviting you to be a part of His great plans for the world. The Bible says God knew you before you were born, before you were even formed in your mother's womb; He knit you together, body and soul (Jeremiah 1:5; Psalm 139:13).

God had a plan for you before you were born. He has already gone all in, knowing you are destined to do something great, something significant, something designed just for you. He just needs you to go all in on Him and commit to following (and following through) whatever the cost.

God has always had a plan for you, and He gave His all to prove it. Do you believe this?

Believe He Has a Plan

Think back to when you were a kid—perhaps you would place a bet with your friends or siblings. Maybe you said something like, "I bet you can't ride your bike down that hill," or "I bet you can't jump that ramp with your skateboard."

As a kid, I was willing to take the risk for the sake of a bet. To this day, I've got the scar to prove that I took the skateboard bet. I took the bet—and even won the bet—but had to suffer the pain of catching my arm on a rusty nail sticking up out of that ramp.

I remember once playing a game of truth or dare, which turned into a bet that I wouldn't take my clothes off and run around the neighborhood in the buff. I took the bet but immediately regretted it once my mom caught me.

Kids sometimes take crazy bets because they believe they can do anything. As they grow older, though, doubt creeps in and confidence fades a bit. They begin to realize they are *not* invincible and start to fear that they don't have the capacity to do what they are asked to do. In fact, one of the biggest fears people have is that they won't measure up to others' expectations.

Christians become terrified at the thought that God wants them to be all in—that no matter what He asks, they have to say yes. They have to accept the "dare." In God's defense, He *knows* we can accomplish great things! But we seldom have that level of confidence.

What if I don't measure up? What if I can't get the job done? What if I can't meet His expectations?

When my family and I first left Florida and moved to California, we had certain expectations and plans. I was betting on things to work out a certain way.

It didn't take long after our move to realize things weren't going exactly as planned. In fact, things weren't going *anywhere near* the way I had planned. I started to doubt myself and my decisions, and I lost confidence in my ability to make things work. I didn't know what to do, and every time I tried a new direction, I seemed to hit a roadblock.

God always has a wonderful sense of timing, though. He also has a wonderful sense of humor. During this time, on top of everything else, God decided to add to our family—and my daughter was born. I remember telling the doctor that, given our situation, we might have to put our daughter on layaway because I didn't know how I would pay for her! But we began working through the situation, keeping in mind that the more I went all in on God, the more He would make a way.

When we first arrived in California, I was betting on myself. But the more I put my stock in God, the more I saw the *real* path He had for me.

I found myself back on active duty in the Navy, and when that ended, we began asking what was next. I didn't have a clue.

But God did. He had a plan for me that He knew I was capable of accomplishing. He called me back to what I was meant to do—work alongside people. His plan for me was to encourage others and help them to grow personally and professionally so that they, in turn, could do great things in this world.

God had a vision for a church I was to lead even before I had a clue. God had a plan for me and that church before I was even formed in my mother's womb. He had a vision for every member of that church as well, just like He had a vision for me, and just like He has a vision for you.

However, we can't buy into God's vision until we first buy into God.

Think about that: *God has huge plans for all people.* In fact, the Bible says, "every knee should bow ... every tongue should confess that Jesus Christ is Lord" (Philippians 2:10–11 NKJV). God is looking forward to a day where there will be no more suffering, no more sorrow, no more pain, and no more tears. It will be a day when people will know how to truly love one another, forgive one another, and care for each other.

It's a huge vision. But that vision won't become a reality until God's people believe in Him.

God believes in you today—right now, right this second. He knows you can fulfill the plans He has for your life; do you trust Him enough to believe He won't fail you when you give Him your all?

Betting with Confidence

Before the Israelites entered the Promised Land, Joshua gave specific instructions for how the people were to prepare for this great act:

> *So it was, after three days, that the officers went through the camp; and they commanded the people, saying, "When you see the ark of the covenant of the LORD your God, and the priests, the Levites, bearing it, then you shall set out from your place and go after it. Yet there shall be a space between you and it, about two thousand cubits by measure. Do not come near it, that you may know the way by which you must go, for you have not passed this way before."*
>
> *And Joshua said to the people, "Sanctify yourselves, for tomorrow the LORD will do wonders among you." Then Joshua spoke to the priests, saying, "Take up the ark of the covenant and cross over before the people."*
>
> *So they took up the ark of the covenant and went before the people.*
>
> *— Joshua 3:2-6 (NKJV)*

The Israelites had never traveled the way God wanted them to go. Joshua commanded the people to follow the ark of the covenant; if they did, God would show the way.

Joshua had seen God work throughout his life.

When he was a young man, God's presence had been with Moses up on the mountain when God had given the Ten Commandments.

During the forty days Moses was up on the mountain, the people had decided they couldn't trust God anymore, or Moses for that matter. Instead, they pooled their gold together, melted it down, and created a golden calf. They were all in on the golden calf, ready to bet on that man-made idol instead of on God.

Joshua was with Moses when Moses returned from the mountain and found the people worshiping the golden idol. Joshua saw that even amid such incredible betrayal, God still had plans for His people.

Joshua knew the Israelites' hearts were rebellious, but he also knew he served a God who continued to use His people to fulfill His plans, even when they turned against Him. Because of this, Joshua was all in with God.

Eventually, Joshua led these same rebellious people into the Promised Land. However, Joshua was not the first Israelite to enter the new territory. The priests, carrying the ark of the covenant high, crossed the Jordan before the people had put one foot in the water.

Recently, at a men's meeting, I showed the attendees a scene from the movie *Braveheart*. In one scene, the priest came out and blessed the people before they went into battle—the priests leading the way.[1]

In ancient times, priests led the battle procession like first responders at a dangerous situation, and the people followed behind. Because priests were God's representatives, this imagery reveals God should be the One who goes before us in our battles.

Joshua had told the Levites—the priests—to take the ark into the water at high tide (Joshua 3:11–17). This was not a good time to cross the Jordan River. The elements were against them. But by asking Joshua to tell the priests to do something risky, God showed that He could be trusted. The people followed based on the trust the priests had in God. If the priests demonstrated complete trust in God by entering the waters at high tide, the people could trust God, too.

Sure enough, the waters of the Jordan ceased to flow and pulled back so that the priests could cross on dry ground!

Later in Joshua 10, Joshua prayed out loud to God on behalf of the people. Israel had been battling the Amorites, chasing them over one hill after another for days. Joshua was near victory, but he knew his enemy would be able to sneak away under cover of darkness. So Joshua called out to God and asked that the sun stand still in the sky.

The Bible says the sun stood still a full day, giving Joshua and the Israelites the advantage they needed.

Through the story of Joshua and the Israelites, God assures us if we trust in Him and let Him fight our battles, victory will be ours.

All or Nothing

Has God given you enough reasons and evidence to go all in with Him? Has God convinced you to place everything you have into His hands and bet everything— your entire life—on Him?

Earlier, I told the story about playing with the house money in Vegas, and that I was willing to keep playing because I knew I had the original twenty-five dollars still in my pocket. It was my safety net. Although a sensible precaution, a gambler would say I wasn't really all in.

One of the most beautiful things that happened for us when we moved from Florida to California was that I lost my safety net. I didn't have a way out if things should go badly—if I lost the house money. I didn't have anything in my back pocket. It was scary, but that experience helped me realize that God really did have my back. I learned to trust in His provision, not my own.

Sometimes I wonder how these same Hebrew people—who had already seen God part the Red Sea so they could cross safely when Pharaoh's army was in pursuit, who had seen water come from rocks and food come down from heaven—could be so doggone stubborn. Wasn't that enough evidence for them?

However, I'm stubborn and bullheaded, too. God has given me enough evidence in my life to trust Him with full confidence. He has proven over and over that He's got my back—and I still struggle with going "all in" at times.

What about you? Consider your life—the people around you, the things you have, and the situations you've experienced. Has God given *you* enough reason to go all in?

God has every intention of using you to accomplish incredible things. Do you believe He will be faithful to do it? Are you only willing to play with the house money, or are you ready to give everything over to God, confident that it will be worth it?

Chapter One Questions

Question: In what ways have you played it safe with your Christian life? What part or parts of your life have you been holding back from God?

_____

_____

_____

_____

_____

_____

_____

_____

_____

_____

_____

Question: Do your plans involve betting on you or on God? In what ways can you open up your life to God's vision?

_____

_____

_____

_____

_____

_____

_____

_____

_____

_____

Question: Think of times in your life when it felt like you lost your safety net. How did God provide in those situations? How has He shown that you can put your full confidence in Him?

_____

_____

_____

_____

_____

_____

_____

_____

_____

_____

_____

_____

Action: Take time to pray and reflect on where you feel God's been calling you to go all in. Make a plan for how you're going to step out in faith. Maybe you are being called to read your Bible daily. Maybe you need to meet your neighbors. Write the steps you can take to answer God's call.

Chapter One Notes

_____

_____

_____

_____

_____

_____

_____

_____

_____

_____

_____

_____

_____

_____

_____

_____

_____

_____

_____

_____

_____

CHAPTER TWO

The Measure of Joy and Generosity

Go your way, eat the fat, drink the sweet, and send portions to those for whom nothing is prepared; for this day is holy to our Lord. Do not sorrow, for the joy of the LORD is your strength.

— Nehemiah 8:10 (NKJV)

I once heard a story about a pastor who was leading a funeral service. He invited people to share a memory of the man who had passed away.

One person stood up and said, "Well, Tim liked ice water." The pastor wasn't quite sure what to do with that statement. The man sat down, and another person stood up and said, "Tim *really* liked ice water."

For some people, this will be their legacy: "He really liked ice tea," or, "He really liked the Miami Hurricanes," or, "Man, he was a diehard Pittsburgh Steeler fan."

But nothing deeper can be said.

You and I both have a legacy to pass on, and it's important to give thought to what we'll be remembered for—as the body of Christ and as individuals.

However, sometimes it's hard to imagine finishing well when difficult circumstances make it near impossible to make it through one day.

When people are joyful in the midst of difficult times, others notice and may even ask why that is. It's an important question because it allows the person going through the trial to go deep within to clarify *what it is that leads them to keep pressing on.*

Hearing why others remain hopeful and engaged during difficulties may lead you to discover that you don't have a "why" that is deep enough to keep you going when things get tough. On the other hand, it may remind you of the things that truly matter in this life and encourage you to continue running your race well.

Focused on the Goal

I love following the Olympics and professional sports because of the stories of perseverance, tenacity, and stubbornness. I also find myself asking the question: Why did these people go through such pain and suffering and even isolation to compete in an event that will be over so quickly?

These athletes train for four years and in a matter of ten—maybe fifteen—minutes, unless they participate in a long competition, it's over. And then they've got to wait another four years before they have a chance to try again. Those of us who are not athletic may find ourselves asking: *Why?*

In 2016, I watched the Summer Olympic Games, and I'll never forget the opening ceremony (one of my favorite parts of any Olympic Games). I was away at a drill weekend, which meant no kids and a bit of privacy. As soon as I watched Team Refugee walk into the stadium, I began to cry.

I wept for a couple of reasons—one, it reminded me of Jesus weeping for Jerusalem before He was to be crucified. He wept because its people were like sheep without a shepherd, and that's what the Team Refugee represented; they were a group of people without a country.

I also wept out of joy and inspiration at how cool it was that the Olympic Federation told those people who didn't have a country that the Federation would be their country. In the spirit of the Olympic Games, the homeless athletes would represent the games themselves—or at least the organization behind the games.

And last, I wept at the crowd's reaction. When Team Refugee marched into the stadium, there was a long, standing ovation for this group of ten athletes with no country. This hit me as an example of people choosing joy in adversity.

Those stateless athletes could easily have thrown in the towel. They could have felt sorry for themselves and become bitter and resentful. But instead, they pressed toward their goal. They were going to make it to the Olympics, even as their worlds crumbled around them.

It was also an example of how the church should respond to welcoming those who come with complex, heart-wrenching baggage. What would happen if we chose to celebrate every single person who walked through our church doors rather than judge them, criticize them, or more commonly, avoid them?

If people without a country, a family, or a sense of belonging came to church and were welcomed with applause, how would their lives be changed?

Sharing Joy with Others

Life is complicated, exhausting, and at times difficult. What if, in the hardest and most difficult seasons of life, you could experience authentic joy? Would that make a difference in how you faced each day?

Peter called the first-century Christians to be prepared to share with others the reason they had such hope and joy when death and destruction surrounded them. He knew people were watching and were going to ask why Christians kept pressing on—and why they still believed. *Why did they still have hope?*

In the same way, when uncertainty, worry, and anxiety surround us, God is calling us not only to hold on to His joy but also to be prepared to share with people *why* we have such joy.

In today's world, it's an incredible thing to see someone trusting Jesus while surrounded by so much negativity. As we're bombarded by the news, politics, or disasters, it's easy to get swept away in all the bad. That's why joy stands out. Friends and family will wonder why we seem so positive when all they can see is the negative.

This doesn't mean putting a fake smile on your face. It means possessing authentic joy that comes from a relationship with Christ. And that relationship stems from holding on to Him when things go wrong, trusting Him to put the pieces together, and surrendering every last bit of ourselves to Him—including those aspects of ourselves to which we desperately desire to cling.

Battered by the Storms of Life

Jesus and His disciples were on a boat on the Sea of Galilee. Jesus had fallen asleep, when a violent windstorm arose, kicking up the waves. The disciples were upset and woke Jesus, saying, "Teacher, do You not care that we are perishing?" (Mark 4:38 NKJV; see also Matthew 8:25). The disciples were terrified, believing they were about to die—while Jesus had peacefully curled up like a little boy in the back of the boat and was snoring away.

Jesus stood up, rebuked the wind, and said to the waves, "Peace, be still!" (Mark 4:39 NKJV). The wind and the waves died down. Jesus had an aura of calm in the storm, and His disciples took notice.

When things appear to go wrong, God calls us to trust in Him. Even when we have sinned, we need to repent, trust, and not give up. After all, He doesn't give up on us.

In the book of Nehemiah, after Israel had been released from captivity and Jerusalem's wall had been rebuilt, Ezra stood on a platform and read from the book of the law—the Torah. While looking around at their demolished city, the people were broken as they realized their ancestors had disobeyed God. Their Promised Land needed to be rebuilt and the rubble cleared away.

Where to even begin reconciling with God? However, Nehemiah declared to God's people, "Do not sorrow, for the joy of the LORD is your strength" (Nehemiah 8:10 NKJV). The Israelites were about to experience a tremendous revival, but it would not occur unless the people embraced the call to be joyful despite their brokenness.

Like the Israelites, we are God's people, chosen to be a light to the nations (Isaiah 49:6; Acts 13:47). Like them, we have not lived up to our potential; we haven't always been the people God called us to be. In their brokenness, Nehemiah told them to rejoice in the strength of the Lord, and so must we.

Jesus is inviting you and me to experience the same calm in the storm, the same joy in the midst of brokenness. It's through this that we can live out the lives God has called us to as Christians.

I know what you're thinking. Sometimes when we are plodding along in our comfort zone, when we are just about holding on to what we believe, and someone introduces to us a big idea that says, "Listen! In this difficult time, I want you to have joy in the Lord!" it may cause frustration.

We want to cry out, "Do you not know how tough things are right now?" The disciples faced this on the water. The Israelites' natural conditioning told them to be afraid, too, as they listened to the book of the law. But Jesus quieted the waves. And Nehemiah reminded them of a bigger plan.

Resting in His Strength

If you're in the midst of a storm and you don't have the inner joy I'm writing about, then it's likely you're trying to survive in your own strength. You're in the boat with Jesus, yelling at Him, "Wake up!" You're convinced He doesn't know how bad things really are and, if He would just lend His ear, you could explain just how desperately you need to be rescued.

But of course, Jesus is well aware of everything going on in your life and mine. He is simply waiting for us to stop relying on our strength and thinking, *Maybe if I adjust the sails just so, and maybe if I start rowing toward shore....* The Lord is waiting for us to exercise our strength in Him, instead.

God told Paul, "My grace is sufficient for you, for My strength is made perfect in weakness" (2 Corinthians 12:9 NKJV). Paul believed these words with everything in him, and *because* he believed them he could respond, "Therefore most gladly I will rather boast in my infirmities, that the power of Christ may rest upon me" (NKJV).

It is only when we are weak and resting in Him that God's strength is revealed.

The greatest example of this happened when Jesus rose from the dead.

Jesus had tried to prepare His disciples for what was to come (Mark 8:31), but even so, they must have felt lost after His death. The Bible tells us they were hiding in fear of the Jewish leaders behind locked doors (John 20:19). They were still meeting, of course. They were still carrying on with things the way they had done when

Jesus was alive. But I can imagine how bleak it must have seemed. Their friend, their Lord, was dead.

However, this hopeless situation soon turned into the greatest victory when they discovered His empty tomb and saw Him alive once again.

In their pain and suffering, they drew closer to one another and to God. And, just as planned, God provided not only the strength but the guidance to know where to go from there.

Christians are "empty-tomb people." Our God is alive, and He wants to help us. We must embrace and believe this. He has overcome everything, and He has promised never to leave us or forsake us.

Reality might show us the opposite. It might make us feel as though we can't trust God to come through because things are *so* bleak or *so* far lost. Yes, we know what the Bible says. Yes, we know God's promise to us. But do we believe it?

When the reality of life collides with God's truth, then we're in for some trouble and real testing. It's in that place that we discover whether we truly believe God is with us.

God desires for you to stop and listen for His voice when you feel overwhelmed, and to remember who you are: you are God's beloved son or daughter, and He will never abandon you. Paul said in Ephesians 2:10 that you are God's "masterpiece" (NLT). He breathed life into you and called you to a higher existence. He has you safely in the palm of His hands (John 10:28). You are resting in His arms. He is pulling you close.

This is what Ezra was reminding the people of in Nehemiah 8. A revival was about to break out because the people were to remember who they were, what they were meant to do, how they were going to do it, and why they were going to do it. The only question that wasn't answered was *when*.

God only called them to listen. He would answer when the Israelites trusted no one else but Him as their only source of strength, courage, and peace—just as He longs to be your strength, courage, and peace, too.

Joy in Brokenness

The Bible is clear: though disease can take the physical body, it cannot take the spirit. But depending on where and how we get our strength, our spirits can be positive or negative. They can be Christlike, or they can be self-serving and ugly.

When we look inward to ourselves for our source of strength, the weight of life can become overwhelming. We start to become burdened by sin, sadness, loss, and negativity.

But when we look outward to God for our strength, we can truly cast our cares on Him. Our yokes become lighter. And we can rejoice even in the midst of great suffering.

When we have a Christlike attitude, there is no room for fear because we are filled with God's love, and, in love, there's no room for fear (1 John 4:18). God's love in us enables us to face fear, disease, or trials and say with confidence, "God is on my side. God loves me. There is no room for being fearful." Claiming a Christlike attitude is what brings joy during brokenness.

Don't get me wrong. It's not always easy to choose joy and to choose God. But it does seem to get easier with practice as God reveals more of Himself.

There are three main takeaways when it comes to choosing joy in your pain or brokenness:

First, joy amid brokenness will determine the way you approach life. Life will be difficult, with ups and downs. There will be victories, and there will be defeats; no one is immune to trials. However, striving to live with Christ's attitude and believing God is on your side will determine how you approach life.

One assignment I had on a ship as a Navy chaplain involved a boss with whom I had tremendous difficulty. But God has called me to share the good news with all people, and at that time it was to Navy officers. I wanted them to know the good news that they matter to God.

I would walk the decks and visit with people with a mantra in my head: *What can my boss do to me? Send me back to the church?* I knew God was on my side and it didn't matter if my boss—or anyone—came against me. It didn't matter if people liked me or hated me. At the end of the day, I knew my "why." I knew the reason I was there, and this motivated me to proclaim the message that those men and women on that ship mattered to God.

This kind of confidence in God is incredibly freeing. Yes, I was facing some obstacles on my journey to do what God wanted me to do. But because I knew I was right where God wanted me to be, I was able to go "all in." And that attitude of joy and certainty in Christ affected everything—including my passion for telling the good news.

When you come across people you would classify as spiritual "enemies," who think differently from how you think, who act differently from how you act, and who have values different from yours, that's when you have profound opportunities to tell them they matter to God. Then you can tell them that, because they matter to God, they matter to you.

Thus, joy amid personal brokenness will cause you to approach life in a profoundly different way—in a way that will make a difference for the Kingdom.

Second, joy during brokenness will determine the way you relate to people. In the past, I would come across people who didn't have the same joy I had, and to be honest, I struggled. However, having joy during brokenness determines how I work with difficult people. It propels me to press on, even though they are challenging. It means I won't give up; I strive to understand where they're coming from and how to help them see the Truth.

Finally, joy in the midst of brokenness determines whether you will finish the race or quit. Often Christians assume that once they put their faith in Christ, life will be a rose garden. Unfortunately, that is not the way life is. If it were, God's Word wouldn't have given so much encouragement regarding pressing through the difficult times.

Christians are called to fight even through tribulations. You, too, are called to press on and finish the race set out for you, so that like Paul you might "finish [your] race with joy, and the ministry which [you] received from the Lord Jesus, to testify to the gospel of the grace of God" (Acts 20:24 NKJV). It won't be easy, but you will never be alone. God will be right by your side.

Trusting that God is with you is what will enable you to walk through those challenges with joy.

Choosing Joy

With an attitude of joy during difficult times, you will be able to finish the race. Paul modeled this, saying, "I have fought the good fight, I have finished the race, I have kept the faith" (2 Timothy 4:7 NKJV).

However, just saying you are a Christian doesn't mean you will automatically be joyful in overwhelming or hard times. Joy is a choice, and you must work for it.

If you haven't experienced a difficult time lately, I promise you—it's coming! When it does, you must choose to fight through it knowing you are not fighting by yourself. You've got a big God, who is fighting for you.

Remember who you are: you are God's beloved son or daughter. Keep pressing on because your divine purpose is to lead as many people as you can in your lifetime to the open, loving arms of Jesus Christ.

The last marathon I ran was the Marine Corps Marathon in Washington, DC, and we were on the downhill side. I was about six miles into the 26.2-mile race when I pulled my left quad muscle.

I don't know if running a mile on a pulled quad muscle is stupid, but I am such a stubborn person that I kept pressing on. I finished the 26.2 miles and hopped in the car to drive home. Jackie drove the car, thank goodness, because I suddenly experienced unbelievable pain shooting through my legs. If I could have put my foot through the firewall, I would have!

I was so committed to finishing that race that nothing was going to stop me—not even my health! Looking back, I can laugh at how foolish I was. But think about it. What if I took that same commitment and dedication to finishing that silly race and applied it each and every day to living out my faith?

And I'm sure I'm not alone in my stubbornness.

What exists in your life that you would pull out all the stops for? It might be a child, a relationship, or a job. You're so committed that you'll do whatever it takes to keep going and to see it through.

What if you applied that same dedication to choosing Christ, choosing joy, and sharing those things with others? What if you refused to let setbacks get in the way, and you pursued Him wholeheartedly?

Imagine what life would look like!

Give Thanks in All Situations

Rejoice always, pray without ceasing, in everything give thanks; for this is the will of God in Christ Jesus for you.
— 1 Thessalonians 5:16–18 (NKJV)

I remember going on a hike with my Marine battalion. We were doing a bunch of switchbacks up in the mountains in California. Normally we would hike for a certain period and break at a water pool for refreshment. But this time the colonel decided he was going to march right past the water pools. He wanted to see the character of his Marines when they were told to keep going on despite the normal pattern. We didn't know how long the hike was going to be or what was still ahead—but those of us who happened to be at the front of the pack knew exactly what the colonel was doing.

We climbed back and forth through those switchbacks, ascending higher and higher. I moved toward the back of the line because I knew what was about to happen. And as we kept going with no rest, some guys began to chuck their packs. They didn't know the purpose of this race or the point behind the colonel's exercise.

The colonel was teaching the battalion that sometimes it's necessary to dig deep, beyond what seems possible, to cross the finish line.

You might think you know what the finish line looks like—you might even think you know where it is—but it goes even beyond what you think. That's what the colonel's message was.

Being a Christian doesn't stop at the age of sixty, and it doesn't start at age twenty. It doesn't end when we're home from work and out of the world's eye, and it doesn't start the moment we set foot inside the church. Being a Christian is a 24/7 gig, and choosing joy and Christlikeness is a 24/7 gig. And many times God asks us to go further in our faith than we had originally expected. He asks for more joy than we think we can offer, and then He asks for more joy after that.

I certainly don't always feel joyful. I have times of slipping up. I've learned that a good measure of my joy is found in how I love other people.

A Change of Heart

Most people can be joyful or grateful *after* coming through a difficult experience. We thank the people who have helped or taken care of us, grateful we've come out alive on the other side. But the Bible teaches that we are to be joyful *in the midst of* difficulties. In fact, Paul said in *all* situations we are to give thanks (1 Thessalonians 5:18). I must confess that when I encounter these kinds of texts in the Bible, I am profoundly impacted by God's standards for Christians!

When a person puts their faith in Christ, there is a different level of expectation. Before I was a Christian, when trials bubbled up I responded in a way that was far from Christlike. Words would come out of my mouth that did not reflect Jesus' character, and I reacted in ways Jesus would never have done. But God has a different expectation for Christians.

When I wasn't a Christian, I could sulk, complain, or whine, and I could blame other people for my misfortunes. I could even get angry at God, shake my fist at Him, and scream, *"What did I ever do to you to deserve this kind of attention?"* However, once I became a Christian, God had a different standard, or expectation, for my life—and He has a different expectation for your life, too.

God didn't tell me verbally that when life got rough, I now needed to react a certain way—with a grateful and generous heart. If He did, I might have asked for a second opinion! Rather, the more I understood what Jesus did for me, my inclination toward generosity naturally increased.

When you become a Christian and things go wrong or don't happen the way you want them to happen, this is when it's critical to live with trust and faith in God. Think about that. This is when it's most important to believe God has your back. You can take your anxieties, worries, burdens, and concerns and hand them to God, who will take care of them for you. He will not abandon you, but will walk side-by-side with you.

This is how God wants you to walk with Him, understanding that when you get knocked down, He will help you stand back up. God, who is victorious, will fight your battles for you. Believe this!

Whatever those battles might be, as you go about your daily life remember that when the world yells names at you, ignores you, or even rejects you, God calls you to love those people generously, regardless.

Loving Generously

Imagine you live in Louisiana and have been impacted by a recent flood, or that you live in California and your house has burnt to the ground from a fire. Someone from the United Methodist Committee on Relief comes to you while you are still reeling from your loss and asks you for a donation to help others who have lost their houses. How would you react?

Would you be excited about that invitation to be generous? Likely your joy would not be overflowing at that moment!

A few weeks ago, I was having a hard time. I was having a yogurt-hitting-the-fan kind of week. And I was far from feeling as though I could turn around and generously love others.

Did I have joy that week? Not a chance.

The proof that you are still walking in joy in difficult times is when you find your generosity *increases* despite the storm swirling around you and no end in sight to the clouds, rain, and winds.

Most people—even Christians—operate in a way that protects the very little they have. This is a "scarcity" mentality; they worry they won't have enough to share with everyone. However, God expects Christians to operate with an "abundance" mentality, with the idea that everything belongs to Him. We are supposed to demonstrate an attitude of generosity *in all* situations, with gratitude for God's provision.

Yes, that may seem near impossible.

Eileen Taylor of Amesbury, Massachusetts, had recently lost her job as a physician's assistant when she decided one Saturday morning to visit her favorite place—Heav'nly Donut Shop.[2]

While in the drive-through at Heav'nly Donut Shop, Eileen decided to pay the bill for the car behind her, inspired by a similar act of kindness someone had shown her the day before. When the next car drove up to the window, they were told their $12 order had already been paid for. They were so inspired by this act, in turn, that they paid for the carload behind them as well.

This "pay it forward" chain of generosity continued until no one else was left in line. In all, Heav'nly Donut Shop counted fifty-five carloads that paid each other's bills. Fifty-five customers had continued the act of generosity Eileen had started amidst her difficult circumstances.

The joy we find while going through difficult experiences is revealed in the level of generosity we display toward others. When life is difficult, if you are more generous than you are when everything is going well, others will take note of your joy.

This is the race set out for us—not *finishing* the race and saying thank you to God for coming through yet again. No, the race we face is one of selflessness and generosity. Of showing love to others no matter how crazy or difficult things get.

While Jeremiah was in prison and facing long-term captivity, God told him to purchase some land:

> Take these deeds, both this purchase deed which is sealed and this deed which is open, and put them in an earthen vessel, that they may last many days. For thus says the LORD of hosts, the God of Israel: "Houses and fields and vineyards shall be possessed again in this land."
> — *Jeremiah 32:14–15 (NKJV)*

Jeremiah was heading into life-long captivity—but

stopped to purchase real estate from his cousin! His here-and-now was not positive. He had some dark days ahead. Yet he trusted God and knew it wasn't the end. By purchasing the land, he was giving thanks for a future day when his people would be allowed to return to their homeland. He was expressing gratefulness before he even saw God's promises come to pass. He believed in God's Word that Israel would one day return to the Promised Land. Now *that* is a race well run!

The book of Hebrews relays many stories about people who walked by faith. The writer of Hebrews recounts the stories of real people who finished the race well, often called "the hall of faith" or "the hall of fame of faith believers." They trusted God for what they could not see.

We, too, can give thanks in trials and tribulations as a declaration of our trust and faith in God. Though it may be difficult in the moment, we can choose to be generous, knowing our moments of struggle won't last forever. For God promises He will guide and direct us to a better future. Like King Solomon, we can trust in the Lord with our whole hearts and not in our own understanding, for "He shall direct [our] paths" (Proverbs 3:5–6 NKJV).

God has a plan for you—not a plan to hurt you, but a plan that gives you a hopeful future (Jeremiah 29:11). Your generosity in difficult times is an expression to God of your gratitude and thankfulness for His provision. Paul exhorted believers, "Always be joyful. Never stop praying. Be thankful in all circumstances, for this is God's will for you who belong to Christ Jesus" (1 Thessalonians 5:16–18 NLT).

Paul did not say be joyful and thankful in ninety percent of situations, but in all situations. I'd like to find the wiggle room in these hard teachings, yet Paul leaves none. Be grateful in all circumstances because doing so expresses your trust in God.

What Will You Choose?

Giving thanks, choosing joy, and loving others generously while in the midst of difficult times does not deny the presence of evil and suffering in the world. Choosing to walk with Christ and reflect His teachings *despite* all the evil and suffering is an attitude that believes love conquers all. Even though things get so bad that it may appear like evil is triumphing, or it may seem like bad people are winning, we continue to move in the direction God leads because we believe love conquers all.

This doesn't discount the reality that life is hard. Hurricanes, floods, tornadoes, earthquakes, asteroids—these can be devastating and absolutely horrific events. But they are not representative of God's nature. This world is not the way God created it, nor is it what He intended for His creation. Natural disasters are signs of a fallen creation, but acts of love, joy, thankfulness, and generosity during those disasters reveal what we believe about God.

And in the end, we want to hear the Father say, "Well done, good and faithful servant" (Matthew 25:23 NKJV). We want to know that our race was well run.

However, we should be careful not to let our generosity be a way for us to show how good we are or how spiritual we've become. Being generous in the midst of difficult times is not about us. It is about our faith, our trust in God—more than that, it's what God expects of those who follow Him.

While Jesus was being beaten, bruised, and humiliated, while He was in the most difficult and darkest hours of His life on earth, He demonstrated tremendous generosity. Putting His pain aside, He said from the cross, "Father, forgive them, for they do not know what they do" (Luke 23:34 NKJV).

To do anything less when going through difficult times fails to imitate Christ. The apostle Peter wrote, "For God called you to do good, even if it means suffering, *just as Christ suffered for you*" (1 Peter 2:21 NLT, emphasis added). Jesus is the perfect example of being generous while in difficulty, and Peter exhorts followers of Jesus to follow in their Savior's steps.

To be called Christian means we are imitating the life and the walk of Christ. Paul said believers should have the attitude of Christ, who gave up everything for humanity (Philippians 2:1–18). Though it is easy to fall back on grace, God calls His children to a higher place with different expectations. There is a lifestyle we are called to embrace—a different way which we are called to live.

There is a different race we are expected to run. Let's not forget Hebrews 12:1, which states: "Therefore, since we are surrounded by such a great cloud of witnesses, let us throw off everything that hinders and the sin that so easily entangles, and let us run with perseverance the race marked out for us" (NIV).

Will you join me in this race? Will you choose joy

and generosity? Will you choose a life set apart?
Your measure as a Christian depends on it.

WORKBOOK

Chapter Two Questions

Question: It can be hard to stay positive when life doesn't seem to be going your way. How can you cultivate an attitude of joy that holds strong even in the most difficult seasons?

_____

_____

_____

_____

_____

_____

_____

_____

_____

_____

Question: Do you operate with a scarcity mentality or an abundance mentality? In what ways can you show gratitude to God and generosity to others even in tough times?

_____

_____

_____

_____

_____

_____

_____

_____

_____

_____

_____

Question: What answer will you give when people wonder why you face challenges and endure hardships with joy, hope, and generosity?

_____

_____

_____

_____

_____

_____

_____

_____

_____

_____

_____

_____

Action: List the areas of your life where you tend to feel overwhelmed. Search your Bible or use a Bible search website to find verses that speak to these areas. Spend time memorizing these verses and post them where you'll see them when you're facing these particular hardships.

Chapter Two Notes

CHAPTER THREE

Taking the High Road

"Teacher, which is the great commandment in the law?"
Jesus said to him, "'You shall love the LORD your God with
all your heart, with all your soul, and with all your mind.'
This is the first and great commandment. And the second
is like it: 'You shall love your neighbor as yourself.' On
these two commandments hang all the Law and the
Prophets."
— Matthew 22:36–40 (NKJV)

Matthew 22:36–40 likely ranks in the top ten most-
quoted Bible verses. On its surface, it seems so straight-
forward, and deceptively simple to do. Loving God and
loving others—how hard could that be?

What Loving Really Means

In Luke's Gospel, Jesus unpacked these "simple"
commandments we read in Matthew 22 a bit more, re-
vealing that loving God and loving others is not easy.
Luke expanded on the concept of love which, according

to Jesus, is a bit more complicated and definitely more challenging than at first glance:

> *But I say to you who hear: Love your enemies, do good to those who hate you, bless those who curse you, and pray for those who spitefully use you. To him who strikes you on the one cheek, offer the other also. And from him who takes away your cloak, do not withhold your tunic either. Give to everyone who asks of you. And from him who takes away your goods do not ask them back. And just as you want men to do to you, you also do to them likewise.*
> *—Luke 6:27–31 (NKJV)*

These words in Luke 6 are part of Jesus' Sermon on the Mount. Jesus climbed up on the side of a mountain and began to teach those who had climbed with Him. In this passage, it's as though Jesus invited those with Him to take the high road—to do more than love those whom they felt were *deserving* of love. Jesus called His disciples to love those who were hard to love—to love their enemies (Matthew 5:44; see also Luke 6:27–36).

Jesus extends the same invitation to each of us. He wants us to understand that Christians who finish well are those who take the high road when dealing with difficult people—those who make us angry, rub us the wrong way, don't share our values, and might be downright hateful. Part of the measure of being a Christian comes down to how we love the unlovable.

Most people have lovable parts, but they also have unlovable parts. Yet God chooses to love everyone, regardless of whether they are worthy of love. He loves people so much that He sent Jesus to suffer and die on the cross so we can have life.

God loved me so much that He sent Jesus to walk slowly through the crowd of hurting people just like me, bringing healing and transformation wherever He went; so that when I finally got to the point of asking the question, "Jesus, am I lovable? Jesus, can I be one of those masterpieces You talk about? Jesus, will You call me 'friend'?" He could say, "Yes."

There were times in my life when I believed God didn't even exist. Then I believed He didn't exist *for me;* He couldn't be interested in me because I didn't have things right in my life. I thought that when I did certain things a certain way, or when I talked and dressed a certain way, then I could ask if Jesus was interested in me.

When I finally got to the point of asking if Jesus could love me, He told me, "I've always loved you. You've always been the apple of my eye. You have always been my beloved son."

God says the same to you. He has loved you always. And, in turn, He wants us to feel the same about others.

I don't have a doctorate degree in loving the unlovable. I share the same struggles you have. I struggle with the same questions—does this mean loving the Osama bin Ladens and Adolf Hitlers of the world? Does this mean loving serial killers and child molesters?

I confess I don't know how to do that yet. And that's okay. It's a goal that we, as Christians, must constantly strive toward. The good news is that Jesus left us with a blueprint for how to get there. He offered Himself as an example of what that kind of love looks like, and He sent the Holy Spirit to guide us on the journey.

Dealing with Difficult People

When I find myself dealing with difficult people and difficult circumstances, I often go back to the words Jesus spoke from the cross: "Father, forgive them; for they know not what they do" (Luke 23:34 KJV). I can almost guarantee that had I been the one on that cross, my words would not have been so generous. I might have said something like, "Oh God, would You beat the living daylights out of these people?" or, "Oh God, would You rain Your holy terror down on them?"

But then again, I'm not Jesus. I can't tell you how to love the rapists and murderers in this world. Hopefully, I will be able to write that chapter someday, as I strive to be more like Him.

But what about the person in your life you just don't like? What about the person who is difficult? Maybe he or she is pretentious or moody, or overly zealous about all the wrong things.

How do we, as Christians, take the high road with those types of people—who rub us the wrong way every single day? It could be a co-worker, a neighbor, a member of Bible study, or maybe even a family member. Or what about the people who are on the opposite side of the political fence or who cheer for the wrong football team?

Our responsibility as Christians is to learn to take the high road with those people. And the more we do that, the more we'll be able to learn how to love and take the high road with people who are much more difficult. When we learn how to take the high road in trivial circumstances, we can grow from there and progress to the more difficult challenges. That is how we grow as Christians.

Perhaps you've noticed that when you have proven yourself faithful in something small, God presents you with a bigger opportunity. How we deal with people is no exception. If you prove yourself faithful with people who annoy you in small ways, that doesn't mean you will get a break from future annoying people. Most likely God will send people into your life who will annoy you in a bigger way.

You may be thinking, "Well, that's something to look forward to, isn't it?"

Actually, it is.

If there was ever an obstacle to keep followers of Jesus from finishing well, it's dealing with difficult people. I honestly believe God puts certain people on this planet whose sole purpose in life is to test believers to see just how much we truly believe in love, grace, and forgiveness. These are the people who really know how to push our buttons, provoking a reaction that is likely anything but Christian.

Here is the funny part, though: the person who might be difficult for me could be you, and the person who might be hard for you might be me! Maybe your nosy neighbor drives you crazy—while at the same time, you are driving him or her crazy with *your* nosiness.

The point is that everyone is difficult. Every one of us. Understanding that fact is the first step in taking the high road. I can almost promise you there is someone in the world who thinks you are difficult. The same is true of me. In fact, I'm such a difficult person that even I don't want to hang out with myself sometimes! However, we must learn to see beyond the things we don't like about others and gain God's perspective—so we can truly walk in love.

It's All About Perspective

Many years ago, I had the opportunity to do some cleanup following Hurricane Andrew. While doing the cleanup work, I also worked with some of the youth in the area. There was one little girl, about seven years old, who could curse up a storm! I wondered how she had learned such a vocabulary.

Many heard the language coming out of her mouth and simply wrote her off as another future delinquent. Instead, I took a picture of her. When I looked at that picture, I tried to picture her in her thirties or forties and where she would be. I didn't picture her as a thug or a criminal. Rather, I saw her from the perspective of potential—the winner of the Nobel Peace Prize, maybe, or a senator, doctor, or teacher.

The great author Stephen Covey set out one specific principle in his book *The Seven Habits of Highly Effective People*[3] that has always stuck with me. It is a principle that applies to dealing with difficult people. He urges us to begin with the end in mind (but make sure you have the right end in mind). Essentially, we are to see things from a different, much broader perspective.

After 9/11, my battalion was the "quick reaction force" battalion. That meant we were the on-call battalion to respond to any kind of threatening situation at airports, nuclear plants, and so forth. I had finished my rotation as the quick reaction force chaplain and was on the downhill side of my assignment as a battalion chaplain. I had about five months left before I would go to my first ship when I received an assignment to be the Second Marines First Regiment battalion chaplain in Virginia.

I figured I could skate by for the last five months of my battalion assignment. I could take it easy and prepare for my move to Virginia. The colonel, however, had other ideas.

He pulled me aside and requested I take care of a certain circle of Marines in our battalion who were not thought of highly. Generally, they were labeled as sick, lame, and lazy. Some were looking for ways to get administrative leave. Others had tested positive for drugs. In other words, this particular group of Marines was on the fast track to leaving the Corps, and they were going to leave with a less than honorable discharge. They were no longer performing and instead were choosing to be difficult for the battalion.

Basically, the colonel wanted me to babysit these men during my last five months. He had been giving them menial tasks, like cutting the grass or pulling weeds, but couldn't even motivate them to do that much. I asked the colonel if I could take those men through the course of *The Seven Habits of Highly Effective People.* It took a little convincing, but eventually, he let me give it a try.

It took some time and effort on my part, but the course gradually transformed their thinking. They took on a new attitude and perspective and became contributing members of the battalion.

I received my first commendation medal from the division for my work with those men. What did I do that made the difference? I started with the end in mind. I recognized them for who they were—Marines—not sick, troublemakers, lazy, or any other label that had been given to them. I called them Marines. I didn't view them from their current position but rather saw their potential and where that potential could take them.

I have strived to adopt that as my approach in every situation I face. I choose not to look at where people are currently, but where I see them going in the process. When dealing with difficult people close to me—those who give me grief or a hard time—I try to see where they are at that moment, but also their potential.

This is the approach Jesus took, and it's the approach He wants His disciples to have. It is the key to dealing with difficult people; it is the key to taking the high road and an example of the measure of our Christianity.

God does not see us as we currently are, but rather through the lens of what we are becoming. He sees our potential. If I see a difficult person as a perpetually difficult person, they will likely *remain* a difficult person. If I see an annoying person as a continually annoying person, if I see an argumentative person as always argumentative, or if I see a negative person as forever negative, then guess what? They will always be that way because I will treat them the way I see them.

However, if I see a difficult person through the lens of Christ, then I will begin to treat that person according to their potential—and changes begin to happen. It is crucial that Christians understand this principle.

God did not see us as the sinners we are. God saw us as the saints we could become. He said, "I love you so much that I gave My life. The depth of My love is proven to you on the cross." He didn't leave anyone out; He gave His life for the whole world because everyone matters to Him.

We All Matter

When I was pastoring my first church, there was a woman who seemed to enjoy giving me a hard time. It could be the middle of August and 120 degrees outside, but the minute she would come into my office my teeth would start to chatter. I wasn't cold—I was terrified of what was going to happen next.

I wanted to take the high road, but it created loads of conflict within me. I wanted to give her a piece of my mind, but I was a young pastor and that wouldn't have made a very good impression. I didn't yet fully understand the principle of seeing her from the point of her potential. Instead, from the minute she stepped into my office, I had a set expectation that she was going to be difficult—and she was.

Looking back, I realize that to truly love her I should have challenged her to respond differently to me. I should have expected her to be more loving and respectful toward me. If I had the courage to see beyond her aggressive façade, I could have asked her what was *really* going on. I likely would have seen her from a different perspective—that she mattered to God and was capable of so much more. Had I done this, our relationship would have been different.

This is an important point: taking the high road means more than biting your tongue. In fact, sometimes it means speaking up! Or at least asking the right questions to get people to open up.

Ask yourself: How can I add value to this person? How can I serve him or her? To do that, you must first see their potential and treat them accordingly. In so doing, not only will you show genuine love by helping them finish well, but also you will end up taking the high road to finishing well. The love you show, in that way, will come back to you.

All people matter to God, even difficult people. Even you. Even me. God calls Christians to help others realize that whoever they are, wherever they come from, and whatever point they are at in their lives, they matter to Him. The truth that all people matter to God is one of the core values of Christianity.

In John's Gospel, Jesus said, "You did not choose Me, but I chose you and appointed you that you should go and bear fruit, and that your fruit should remain" (John 15:16 NKJV). Jesus affirmed that God chose us and gave us a job—an "appointment." Even those who have tried to run from God—who have ignored Him or denied Him—He pursued because He chose them for a purpose. And, in turn, He wants His disciples to bear fruit.

Bearing fruit means cultivating others, even those who are difficult and may not be immediately receptive to God's calling. Disciples are called to present God's message, not only to likable people with similar interests but to all people. Disciples are called to serve and see the potential in everyone and to treat them like they matter. All people matter to God, and therefore all people should matter to us.

This perspective may not come instantaneously, but as we climb with Christ it will become more natural for us to take the higher road, and the measure of our Christianity will show through.

It's All About the Climb

In his book *Winning with People*, John C. Maxwell recounts a fable about a combative skunk who taunted and insulted a lion in an unsuccessful effort to pick a fight with the larger beast. Exasperated, the skunk wondered why the lion would refuse to take on such an easy challenge. The lion observed that regardless of who won the fight, the skunk's reputation would grow for fighting a lion, but his reputation would suffer from lowering himself to the level of a skunk.[4]

When we choose to take the high road, we choose to rise above the stink of our human way of doing things. In so doing, we call others into a higher way of existence as well.

When we as Christians choose the high road, our actions eventually bring out the best in those around us—even those who are rude, obnoxious, or just plain difficult. They will begin to change, or at the very least *our perspective* will change so that we see the good in them—the potential they have—even if they can't see it.

This is one of the measures of Christianity; this is what it means to be a Christ-follower.

The first step in loving the unlovable is realizing where that kind of love comes from. God loved us even when we were unlovable, while we were still sinners. He loved us before we ever accepted Jesus as our Savior. He loves us even when we succumb to sin and when we do things we know are wrong.

Human beings cannot fathom that kind of unconditional, all-encompassing love. That kind of love originates from God, and He has appointed His disciples to be channels so that His unconditional love can flow to others.

The only way we can love others with this divine love is through the Holy Spirit. Our knee-jerk reaction, when faced with a difficult person, is to be difficult right back, or maybe just avoid them altogether.

But if we respond to that person in love, relying on God's love that indwells us through the Holy Spirit, then we can see that person through God's eyes. With the Holy Spirit's help, we can see that person's potential and love them and treat them accordingly, knowing that, difficult or not, that person matters to God.

As Jesus was being led to the cross, the crowds mocked Him, jeered at Him, and humiliated Him. On either side of Jesus, two criminals were also being crucified. One criminal mocked Him and called Him names, but the other came to Jesus' defense and rebuked the one who was mocking Him.

Choosing the high ground causes something supernatural to occur. Rude and obnoxious people begin to transform. Taking the high ground begins the moment we realize that the way we treat people is a statement about ourselves; it's a statement about what we truly believe about the value of other people.

Taking the high ground is not easy. It's important to recognize that when Jesus spoke those words about loving our enemies, He was literally standing on high ground. He was on a mountain.

If you want to hear Jesus, grow in your relationship with Him, and become more like Him, you must be willing to make the climb. But climbing a mountain is not easy.

It will take effort to reach that higher ground.

It will require loving people who seem unlovable.

It will require ignoring the bad attitudes people may display *today* and realizing that through Christ they can be different *tomorrow*.

And it will require recognizing that all people, even those who have done terrible, terrible things, matter to God.

It's a long road up this mountain, but the reward is great—for it will lead you to the heart and the mind of God.

Chapter Three Questions

Question: What are some occasions in your life when you went with your initial reaction and responded to someone in an unloving way? Looking back, what could you have done to behave in a more Christlike way?

_____

_____

_____

_____

_____

_____

_____

_____

_____

_____

_____

_____

Question: Think of three people in your life whom you find difficult. What is at least one good quality each of these people possesses? In what specific ways will you start bringing out the best in each person?

_____

_____

_____

_____

_____

_____

_____

_____

_____

_____

_____

_____

Question: Think of at least one person in your life whom other people tend to write off or label as hopeless. What could you do, starting today, to show this person that he or she matters to God?

_____

_____

_____

_____

_____

_____

_____

_____

_____

_____

_____

Action: Instead of focusing on what you don't like about other people, start cultivating their potential according to their value in God's eyes. Consider who is in your life right now who might need to see God's love in a tangible way. Ask God to help you see that person's needs more clearly and to help you find ways to step into that person's life to show him or her love.

Chapter Three Notes

_____

_____

_____

_____

_____

_____

_____

_____

_____

_____

_____

_____

_____

_____

_____

_____

_____

_____

_____

_____

_____

_____

_____

CHAPTER FOUR

Living Like Discovered Treasure

Again, the kingdom of heaven is like treasure hidden in a field, which a man found and hid; and for joy over it he goes and sells all that he has and buys that field.
— Matthew 13:44 (NKJV)

Imagine you just received a check for $85 million. What are the top things you would do with that check?

Would you buy a new house—a mansion, perhaps?

Would you buy that new car and cutting-edge smartphone you've been wanting?

Would you pay off some old bills and your credit card balances?

Would you invest in the stock market?

Would you invest in your home church?

Now, what if the check were for $1 million? Would your top financial priorities be the same? Would the amount change your decision?

The $85 million number is not a random figure I pulled out of the air. People often retire at the age of sixty-five and live to be about eighty years old. Some die younger, and some live past one hundred, but the average person lives for fifteen years beyond their retirement.

And, generally, we are told that to have enough money for that retirement, we should have $1 million saved up. Some of us end up having more, and some end up having less. But the general aim is that $1 million.

Think about that. Each of us is striving to have a monetary value of $1 million by the time we hit sixty-five years old. Now, not everyone will meet that goal and, of course, it isn't discretionary income for those who have achieved it.

However, let's say between eighty and ninety people show up to worship services at my church—or an average of around eighty-five people. That means there could be a value of approximately $85 million sitting in those pews!

But do you know what the problem is? Most people don't believe they are worth $1 million, much less $85 million.

I don't know about your church, but we certainly don't believe there is $85 million in the sanctuary on Sunday morning, because we don't act like an $85 million church. And because we don't act like an $85 million church, we don't have the impact or the influence of an $85 million church in our community or around the world.

But I believe we have the *potential* of acting that way. Regardless of whether or not our congregation has this sort of money, God has unlimited resources. It starts with remembering what the most important asset of a church is: people. Relationships matter, but a church must first discover what it's worth before it can begin acting on its worth.

Investing Your Treasure

If you discovered you had a treasure worth millions of dollars, you'd likely celebrate—even if you were the only one celebrating!

There is a story in the Bible about a man who discovered a treasure in a field. He sold all that he had to buy the field (Matthew 13:44).

In another story, a merchant was looking for "beautiful pearls" (Matthew 13:45 NKJV). He "found one pearl of great price" and then "went and sold all that he had and bought it" (Matthew 13:46 NKJV).

The Bible says, "From everyone who has been given much, much will be demanded; and from the one who has been entrusted with much, much more will be asked" (Luke 12:48 NIV). Or, as Spiderman's Uncle Ben puts it, "With much power comes much responsibility."[5]

Sometimes responsibility is scary. If God says the church I pastor is an $85 million church, then that must mean I am expected to produce an $85 million ministry in the process.

When your time on earth comes to an end, will you be able to show that what you did with your life was worth millions of dollars? Will you have used your treasure to connect hundreds, if not thousands, of people to the amazing power and love of Jesus Christ?

You will if you claim three truths.

Truth #1. It is easier to be generous and take risks with someone else's money. If you call yourself a Christian, you know that death is not the end but rather the beginning. There is no end for Christians, who will live for eternity. Death only brings an end to the chaos and craziness of this present world. It brings an end to brokenness and imperfection, and ushers in the perfect world God has prepared for those who love Him.

To be quite honest with you, I am a person who saves, as the saying goes, "for a rainy day." I try to be practical, pragmatic, and responsible with money, saving extra when I can in case I ever need it. But what I'm really doing is saving up for a rainy day *hoping that there will not be a rainy day.*

As we saw earlier, the Bible recounts the story of how the Hebrew people were out in the wilderness with no food, and God provided manna from heaven to sustain them. However, He told the Israelites not to collect manna on the Sabbath. They were not to save up for a rainy day. They were to trust God to provide for their needs.

But some wanted to be super-responsible. They wanted to be pragmatic and do what seemed like the right thing—so they gathered up manna "for a rainy day," or for the Sabbath. But when they opened their containers, the manna had spoiled.

There is a tension that exists for us. It's okay to earn and save all that you can, but it's the purpose that matters most. Earning and saving should be for *giving all that you can.*

God wants His people to realize they need not be afraid of running out of food. If you grew up in a household where it was a real possibility you might not have enough food for the next day, you might still have that mentality; you might save certain things because you don't know when those things won't be available.

But the Bible teaches that God always provides. Our job is to recognize that God does not provide resources to prolong our lives or make us feel comfortable, safe, and secure. Rather, God provides these resources to connect people with His amazing power and love.

We are truly living like we are worth millions of dollars when we are connecting as many people as we can to this love. And we can only do this when we remember God owns everything. It's His money we're spending. It's as if He is cutting us a blank check. The kicker? He wants us to cash it.

Truth #2. Choosing to invest rather than spend will result in more bang for your buck. Investing in buildings and properties brings some return on investments, but investing in people and relationships multiplies the gifts God has given a thousandfold.

Consider my small ministry alone. I've been engaged in intentional ministry since 1987. Let's say that over the past thirty years, I have connected the message of God and His love and grace with one hundred people each year—which makes three thousand. Imagine that every year, ten of those one hundred people connected to other people, and they connected to ten other people.

That would mean tens of thousands of people have learned of God's love through me alone. And as time goes on, it grows exponentially. My investment in one person can end up impacting hundreds, if not thousands or more!

One person makes a difference. When we live like we are worth millions of dollars and choose to invest in people, we have the potential to connect thousands of individuals to God's amazing love and power.

Truth #3. Living like you are worth millions of dollars has a far-reaching impact. You will connect thousands of people to God's amazing love and power when you understand that God believes you are His best investment. The man who found the treasure in the field and the man who found the great pearl sold everything to gain the right to the treasure. Those parables are about God who found His treasure: *you*. God loves you so much that He humbled Himself and became obedient to death on the cross to set you free—to gain the right to the treasure.

God's Treasure

God died for you because you are a treasure. In fact, in Malachi we read what God said about all those who follow Him: "'They shall be Mine,' says the LORD of hosts, 'On the day that I make them My jewels. And I will spare them as a man spares his own son who serves him'" (Malachi 3:17 NKJV).

When God created Adam and Eve He called His creation "very good" (Genesis 1:31 NKJV). You, too, are "very good," His most prized treasure in the garden. But that treasure was lost when Adam sinned. Man became like the lost coin, the coin the woman desperately searched to find (Luke 15:8–10). When she did, she rejoiced. God has sought to find you, too.

God is like the father of the prodigal son. Every day the father ran to the edge of town looking for his lost son (Luke 15:11–32). God is like the shepherd who had a hundred sheep. When one sheep was lost, the shepherd searched relentlessly until he found it (Luke 15:3–7). That's who God is—He searches for the lost. With the death of His Son, Jesus, God purchased the right to search for you, His treasure in Jesus, because you are His best investment. You are His masterpiece. Therefore, live life according to what God says you are worth. Live like you are worth millions of dollars.

Disciples within the body of Christ will reach thousands of people when we realize and appreciate that God believes we are the best investment He could ever make. The sooner we see this and believe it, the sooner we measure up to the life to which Christ is calling us.

Chapter Four Questions

Question: What resources has God entrusted specifically to you?

_____

_____

_____

_____

_____

_____

_____

_____

_____

_____

_____

Question: How are you currently using those resources?

_____

_____

_____

_____

_____

_____

_____

_____

_____

_____

Question: What changes will you make to start using what God provides to connect people to His amazing power and love?

_____

_____

_____

_____

_____

_____

_____

_____

_____

_____

_____

_____

Action: Even if you don't feel that you have a lot of ex-tra income, there are ways you can begin to be generous. Consider setting aside a small amount of money each month that can only be used to help those in need. Start a "coffee time" fund that you must use to meet with people in your life who might need to talk. Or take a biblical step and start tithing.

Chapter Four Notes

_____

_____

_____

_____

_____

_____

_____

_____

_____

_____

_____

_____

_____

_____

_____

_____

_____

_____

_____

_____

_____

_____

_____

CHAPTER FIVE

Blessed to Be a Blessing

Then one from the crowd said to Him, "Teacher, tell my brother to divide the inheritance with me." But He said to him, "Man, who made Me a judge or an arbitrator over you?" And He said to them, "Take heed and beware of covetousness, for one's life does not consist in the abundance of the things he possesses."
— Luke 12:13–15 (NKJV)

Have you ever subscribed to the Publishers Clearing House sweepstakes? The advertisements on television are well known. A van shows up at a person's door, and a man with flowers, balloons, and a huge cardboard check knocks, ready to change someone's life. I have signed up—I figure if I'm going to read those magazines anyway, I might as well win a million dollars in the process.

Here Comes the Prize Patrol!

Imagine for a moment that somewhere in your

hometown, maybe right down the street from you, someone woke up this morning and discovered they had won $487 million. Think about that.

Or suppose one Sunday morning in church, the pastor stood up and said that during the week he received a phone call from Publishers Clearing House Prize Patrol telling him that someone in the congregation won the Grand Prize. The Prize Patrol wanted to present it to the winner in church on Sunday.

How hard would your heart be beating at that point? Would you be sneaking a peek at the various doors, trying to spot the van outside one of the windows?

What would you do if at that moment, while the pastor was still speaking, the Prize Patrol burst through the doors, balloons in hand, and headed right to where you were sitting? Suppose they smiled as they locked eyes with you and started walking toward you. It's evident you are about to receive an abundant blessing—how would you react?

Of course, you would be excited! Who wouldn't be?

Now, suppose that, as your heart beats faster and your mind races about what to say, the Prize Patrol walks right past you to the person sitting next to you. They weren't looking at you after all.

Remember, you are in church. How would you feel? Disappointed? Jealous? Maybe you would think to yourself that the person next to you is more blessed than you. They won the money; you didn't. Maybe you'd remember you couldn't win the prize because you never entered the drawing. The person next to you did, and they received the blessing.

Now, let's take things a step further. Suppose the person next to you had proven to be not very responsible. Perhaps they showed themselves to be immature, or maybe they were not such a nice person. Maybe they didn't step up and help at the church as you did, or maybe they were just mean-tempered. Yet they received the check; they received the blessing, not you. Would that make you doubly disappointed?

Winning Is Only the Beginning

Next, imagine you won the big prize. It's all for you! But, what if I told you there was a catch—a condition to enjoying the benefit of your winnings?

With that in mind, let's look at one of the stories in Luke's Gospel:

Someone in the crowd said to Him [Jesus], "Teacher, tell my brother to divide the inheritance with me."

Jesus replied, "Man, who appointed me a judge or an arbiter between you?" Then he said to them, "Watch out! Be on your guard against all kinds of greed; life does not consist in an abundance of possessions."

And he told them this parable: "The ground of a certain rich man yielded an abundant harvest. He thought to himself, 'What shall I do? I have no place to store my crops.'

"Then he said, 'This is what I'll do. I will tear down my barns and build bigger ones, and there I will store my surplus grain. And I'll say to myself, "You have plenty of grain laid up for many years. Take life easy; eat, drink and be merry."'

> *"But God said to him, 'You fool! This very night your life will be demanded from you. Then who will get what you have prepared for yourself?'*
>
> *"This is how it will be with whoever stores up things for themselves but is not rich toward God."*
> — *Luke 12:13–21 (NIV)*

The question at the core of Luke 12:13–21 is: Are you a blessing to others?

On the surface, in this passage, Jesus appeared to be addressing the issue of coveting and greed. "Coveting" is not a typical word in twenty-first-century conversation, except maybe in the Bible or in church. To covet something means we want to possess it. Or, if we already have it, we want *more* of it.

I am a preacher. I look for the opportunity to preach the gospel—to have folks come and sit in church on Sunday morning and hear me share a message of God's love and grace.

But suppose I begin looking around at other preachers and notice their crowds are bigger than my crowds. Suddenly, I want my crowds to be as big as theirs, maybe bigger, or even to have some of their people come to my church. I want to have as much influence, insight, and abundance as they have. That is coveting.

Some might say there's nothing wrong with that; it's just good, healthy ambition. That's what I used to think, and I would justify my planning and strategizing as a demonstration of my enthusiasm. However, Luke 12 declares that what I was doing was clearly coveting—seeking more for myself, not for others.

God was willing to sacrifice everything for you. You have won the Grand Prize because of His love and grace, and the Prize Patrol in the person of Jesus has shown up on your doorstep. But to experience fully the prize He is offering, you must be a blessing to others. Simply put, believers are blessed to be a blessing.

It's All About Me, Right?

Several years ago, I took my family to Disney World. A grandmother just about ran my daughter over trying to help her granddaughter see Cinderella. I decided to talk to this grandmother about her behavior. Well, the woman hadn't even realized what she had done. At that moment, with thousands of people around pressing in on her, she saw only one person—Cinderella. She wasn't trying to be rude or mean but was so focused on reaching Cinderella that nothing else mattered.

That's what was happening with Jesus in that passage in Luke 12. Thousands had gathered, and Jesus was in the process of teaching. He was giving the crowd a list of warnings, of dos and don'ts. The people wanted to hear His every word and didn't want to miss a thing. So they leaned forward, nudged their way closer, and pushed their way past others in the crowd.

At that point, Jesus was talking about the religious leaders—the Pharisees and scribes—and He had just told the story about the good Samaritan. Then, out of nowhere, a man stepped up and said, "Teacher, tell my brother to divide the inheritance with me" (Luke 12:13 NIV).

Perhaps Jesus was put off at the interruption, or perhaps He wasn't bothered at all. But what about the other people listening? Jesus was teaching a riveting story, relaying crucial, life-changing information, when a man interrupted with his own petty issue that had nothing to do with what Jesus was teaching. The crowd was likely irritated.

Jesus' response reflected the situation. He said to the man, "Who appointed me a judge or an arbiter between you?" (Luke 12:14 NIV). Basically, Jesus told the man, "What I am talking about right now has nothing to do with what you want to talk about. Go find a lawyer."

But then, Jesus seized the opportunity to turn the rude interruption into a teaching point, and it was something people can connect with in this generation. While on the surface it appears that Jesus was teaching about coveting and greed, a closer look reveals that the story teaches so much more.

Jesus continued: "Watch out! Be on your guard against all kinds of greed; life does not consist in an abundance of possessions" (Luke 12:15 NIV). It would seem obvious that there is more to life than just possessions, but Jesus didn't stop there. He wanted to transform the perspective of the man who interrupted him, and He wanted to transform our perspective as well. He did so by telling that parable of a man with a full storehouse.

Jesus' parable spoke to the heart of the individual. It was designed not only to teach the crowd of thousands but also to change the heart of one man.

In the parable, the man was a recipient of a bumper crop. In fact, he had such an abundance of crops that he decided to build extra barns to hold it all. He saved so much in his barns and storehouses that he said to himself, "Now I can sit back and relax, take it easy, and enjoy my abundance."

The Prize Patrol had shown up at his house, and the man now had more than he knew what to do with. He made the same decision many of us might make if we found ourselves on the receiving end of a windfall—spend some, save some, quit our jobs, and live a life of leisure. Those seem like logical decisions, right?

But this man apparently made one very foolish decision. In fact, God called him a fool! He probably worked hard to grow his crop and perhaps was lucky that year because the weather was just right, or the ground was in great condition.

Regardless, he still had to work the crops to make them grow. The man was finally able to relax and sit back to enjoy the fruits of his labor. In modern terms, it was time for him to retire and enjoy the savings stashed away in his retirement account.

Consider this parable in terms of church life. Suppose you are with a church that has struggled for many years but now has come into its own, with 700,000 members who tithe on a regular basis. The church coffers are overflowing. The pastor sits back and decides it's time to relax a little and enjoy the fruits of his long years of labor.

According to Jesus' parable, this would be a foolish decision—for as soon as he rested, the man in the parable stopped producing.

Blessings Are Meant to Be Shared

The man in the parable looked back at everything he had and decided he didn't have to produce any more. But the story Jesus told was not really about the man with the bumper crop. Jesus was addressing the man who interrupted Him—the man who, surrounded by thousands of people, could think only about himself.

Through the parable, Jesus invited the man who interrupted—and us as well—to consider the heart of the man who had the bumper crop. What was his personality like?

Six times in that passage alone Jesus used the pronoun "I," and four times He used the pronoun "my" to communicate the man's focus. In those three verses, the man with the bumper crop referred to himself eleven times!

Not once did the man express concern for anyone else. The man never said, "I am so blessed. How can I share this blessing with others?" Not once did he consider how he could help his family, his friends, or his community with the abundance he had been blessed with.

It is hard to be a blessing when all you think about is yourself. That is true for individuals, the church, and nations. Your blessings will be buried with you if you think the blessings you have belong only to you. Churches will die if they believe their blessing belongs only to them. Nations will be turned upside down and destroyed if they believe their blessings belong only to them.

Every person who calls himself or herself a Christ-follower is blessed, but that blessing will be buried if it's not shared with others.

I once watched a video put out by the Make-A-Wish Foundation. Landry, the little boy in the video, was born with a serious condition that required him to undergo brain surgery at a young age. Landry was a loving child and had a personality to which everyone was drawn.[6]

When he was approached by Make-A-Wish, he wished for a treehouse—but not just any treehouse. He wanted one big enough to share with everyone, with his family and friends. He asked his friends and the kids in the neighborhood to write down what they would want to see in the treehouse, and he had Make-A-Wish design one that would fulfill everyone's wishes, not just his own.

Landry had discovered at a young age that life is fragile. He discovered that, at any moment, his life could be changed forever. He didn't want the treehouse to be a blessing just for him; he wanted it to be a blessing for everybody. He even made it accessible for his dogs so they could enjoy the treehouse, too!

The whole neighborhood gathered around Landry to celebrate that treehouse. Landry chose not to bury his blessings, but to share them.

I imagine if the man in the parable knew how soon he was going to die, he might have made some different choices. Unfortunately, he was so wrapped up in his own world that he couldn't see the thousands of people around him. He couldn't see that the bigger picture wasn't all about him, and as a result, he couldn't operate that way. His blessing was buried with him, and he cheated himself out of being a blessing in the process.

Our days on this planet are numbered. We don't know when we will reach the end of that countdown. As Christians, we should be compelled to ask the question: What should I do with the abundance God has already provided?

In 1987, a spiritual prize patrol showed up on my doorstep, and it came in the form of Chaplin Mosley. Chaplin Mosley baptized me, and as he brought me up out of the water, he said, "Tim, meet your family. Family, meet your brother."

Now, I didn't know how much wealth I had been given at that moment; I didn't quite grasp the immensity of the prize. But over time, as I unpacked certain things, I realized the value of what I had been given. I allowed that knowledge to enter my heart, and my heart was transformed.

Among the wealth I received was the knowledge that I was one of God's beloved children and, as such, I was blessed to be a blessing to others.

This prize patrol is knocking on your door, too. It may have already knocked, and perhaps you have already discovered the blessing you are. You may have heard and embraced the truth that you are God's masterpiece and His beloved child.

The question is: What will you do with that blessing? Will you, in turn, be a blessing to others? Or will your blessing be buried with you?

God is calling us to be generous, to bless others, and to give out of the greatness given to us. Will you heed that call? Will you measure up?

WORKBOOK

Chapter Five Questions

Question: What are some ways God has blessed you?

_____

_____

_____

_____

_____

_____

_____

_____

_____

_____

Question: Consider all the people you come into contact with throughout the day. Who could benefit from your blessings?

_____

_____

_____

_____

_____

_____

_____

_____

_____

_____

Question: Now think even bigger. How could you start investing your blessings to benefit people you haven't even met?

_____

_____

_____

_____

_____

_____

_____

_____

_____

_____

_____

_____

_____

Action: Make a list of people in your life who could use a blessing. Watch these people for an opportunity to step in and show them God's love. Make notes on your original list to keep track of who it is that you've blessed. Add new names to the list as often as you can.

Chapter Five Notes

_____

_____

_____

_____

_____

_____

_____

_____

_____

_____

_____

_____

_____

_____

_____

_____

_____

_____

_____

CHAPTER SIX

How Do You Measure Up?

Did you like tests in school? How about pop quizzes? I had a teacher who loved to give pop quizzes. Any time we had a break from school, whether a three-day break or a longer break like Christmas, Miss Bush would promptly administer a pop quiz the day we came back. I am not kidding—the day before I graduated from high school, she gave us a pop quiz. Miss Bush was not one of my favorite teachers.

The Navy seems to like pop quizzes as well. We would be preparing for a conference, and our commanding officers would administer a quiz at the beginning to prove how much we didn't know. After sitting through the conference, we would have to take another quiz to prove how much we learned from the conference.

The objective of a quiz or exam is to measure how much someone has learned and to measure how well faculty has taught. When someone doesn't do well on an exam or quiz, I always believed it had nothing to do with their ability to learn and everything to do with the teacher's ability to teach.

And then I married a teacher.

Since then I have changed my tune. Common Core is meant to establish a certain set of criteria for the entire nation. The idea is that a third grader in one state knows the same thing a third grader in any other state knows. It allows math and reading comprehension to be measured. Sermon feedback does the same thing—the pastor is looking to see if certain criteria were met based on the responses.

In the military, there is a phrase often used: "What gets measured gets done." If you want students to perform well in school, give them a book report that measures whether they read the book or not.

What if we took this same approach and applied it to how we love?

Knowing What's Expected of Us

In the summer, before any one of my children enters school, I sit down with them to discuss the upcoming school year.

In this meeting, I tell them they will be going into a "foreign land" where many children come from different directions and walks of life, with different experiences. I tell them this land will also have giants called teachers. I tell them that when they go into this land, there is a certain way in which they need to conduct themselves.

In all of my direction and advice, I am of course hopeful they will remember who they are—their mommy and daddy's beloved son or daughter. I want them to remember they are the apple of our eyes.

But I also want them to follow my instruction so they will survive! They need to have compassion and care for fellow classmates. They need to add value to others' lives. They need to do their very best in all things, even when they don't like the subject or the work.

This is what Moses was saying to his people in Deuteronomy 6: Remember who you are. You are God's beloved son or daughter. You are the apple of God's eye. You are God's masterpiece.

> *Now this is the commandment, and these are the statutes and judgments which the LORD your God has commanded to teach you, that you may observe them in the land which you are crossing over to possess, that you may fear the LORD your God, to keep all His statutes and His commandments which I command you, you and your son and your grandson, all the days of your life, and that your days may be prolonged. Therefore hear, O Israel, and be careful to observe it, that it may be well with you, and that you may multiply greatly as the LORD God of your fathers has promised you—"a land flowing with milk and honey."*
>
> *— Deuteronomy 6:1–3 (NKJV)*

But more than that, Moses was preparing them to enter a foreign land. To help them, he also revealed how they were (and how we are) supposed to live.

> *Hear, O Israel: The LORD our God, the LORD is one! You shall love the LORD your God with all your heart, with all your soul, and with all your strength.*

And these words which I command you today shall be in your heart. You shall teach them diligently to your children, and shall talk of them when you sit in your house, when you walk by the way, when you lie down, and when you rise up. You shall bind them as a sign on your hand, and they shall be as frontlets between your eyes. You shall write them on the doorposts of your house and on your gates.

So it shall be, when the LORD your God brings you into the land of which He swore to your fathers, to Abraham, Isaac, and Jacob, to give you large and beautiful cities which you did not build, houses full of all good things, which you did not fill, hewn-out wells which you did not dig, vineyards and olive trees which you did not plant—when you have eaten and are full—then beware, lest you forget the LORD who brought you out of the land of Egypt, from the house of bondage. You shall fear the LORD your God and serve Him, and shall take oaths in His name. You shall not go after other gods, the gods of the peoples who are all around you (for the LORD your God is a jealous God among you), lest the anger of the LORD your God be aroused against you and destroy you from the face of the earth.

You shall not tempt the LORD your God as you tempted Him in Massah. You shall diligently keep the commandments of the LORD your God, His testimonies, and His statutes which He has commanded you. And you shall do what is right and good in the sight of the LORD, that it may be well with you, and that you may go in and possess the good land of which the LORD swore to your fathers, to cast out all your enemies from before you, as the LORD has spoken.

— Deuteronomy 6:4–19 (NKJV)

We are to love God with all our heart, soul, and strength (verse 5). We are to adhere to the Ten Commandments and teach them to our children (verses 6 and 7). We are not to forget the Lord and all He has done (verse 12). We are to fear the Lord and serve only Him (verse 13). And we are never to put Him to the test (verse 16).

These are five things that God expects from us.

How do you measure up?

Know Who You Are

Our capacity to adhere to these principles is dependent upon our sense of identity—knowing who we are in Christ.

God told the Israelites to remember who they were before they crossed into the Jordan. The Israelites were once slaves but were now a free people delivered by the hand of God. He reminded them they were a people chosen by Him to reveal His power to the world. He called them to conduct themselves in a way that showed other nations they worship and serve a big God. That would be the Israelites' legacy.

Our situation is vastly different, but we face similar pressures. You, too, will be surrounded by people who worship many gods—whatever they choose to honor and glorify in their lives—while you stand firm and believe there is only one God. You have the choice not to submit to any other god but Yahweh. You may not face war and bloodshed, but there will be opposition, and maybe even threats and intimidation.

However, in all that God expects from you, in all that the world will throw at you, your capacity to rise above and to succeed at each of these five principles is determined by how you love God and how you love others.

Covenantal Love

In the Bible, the word *love* comes from the Hebrew word *hesed*.[7] Hesed involves two different loves: covenant love and sacrificial love. When we talk about measuring our love, we are talking about hesed love.

Covenantal love involves something like a contract. When one contracts with a person, they likely make copies of the contract. If one party breaks the contract, the other party can go back and review their copy of the agreement. The breach of contract is typically very clear, and they can measure that breach based on what the original agreement states.

Moses exhorted the Israelites to allow God to be their protector and fight for them. He descended Mount Sinai after receiving the Ten Commandments on two tablets. These commandments were God's contract with Israel. It was God saying, "Hey, you follow these stipulations, and I will come through for you again and again."

However, God didn't write five commandments on one tablet and five on the other. When Moses descended Mount Sinai, he was carrying two contracts—God's contract and the people's contract. These subsequently went into the ark of the covenant so the people would remember that God's love would always be with them.

The commandments represent God's love, God's contract with His people. Later the prophet Jeremiah wrote about a new kind of contract:

> *But this is the covenant that I will make with the house of Israel after those days, says the LORD: I will put My law in*

their minds, and write it on their hearts; and I will be
their God, and they shall be My people.
— Jeremiah 31:33 (NKJV)

One day, God would write His law on His people's hearts. This would be their passion, what motivated them to get up in the morning. It is what would drive God's people when they didn't feel like taking that next step.

I am a runner; it's part of the way I deal with stress and stay focused. There are plenty of times I don't feel like running, but I've made a promise—a covenant—to myself. So I must run—come rain, heat, or humidity. When I don't follow that promise, I pay a price.

Sometimes I run at the gym, and any gym rat will tell you that January and February are the worst months to work out. It's packed with people who have good intentions and have made promises to themselves to get into shape or train for a race, but do you know what happens come March? Most of those people are gone.

God wants to know if you have covenant love for Him. Covenant love means you don't break your promises. It means you are a promise keeper.

He wants to know that you're going to stay true to your commitment and remember your promise to follow Him, even if it means loving the unlovable, finding joy in hardship, and being generous when you only want to be selfish.

A Challenge

I challenge you to develop the basic habit of being a

promise keeper. First, spend five minutes a day reading your Bible. Next, commit to attending church regularly and bringing your Bible with you. Third, when you wake up in the morning, commit to telling God you love Him before you get out of bed. And when you go to bed at night, commit to saying, "Good night, God. I love you." If you are a checklist-oriented person, write these promises down and check them off each and every day. These are simple ways to start measuring love. They may seem ridiculously simple, but when you do the little things and keep simple promises to yourself, you will have a stronger sense of who you are and your capacity to adhere to the big promises of loving God and loving others.

God wants to know that you think about Him throughout the day. If you want to hear from God, read His Word. Committing to reading for just five minutes a day shows God how much you love Him.

Soon that five minutes a day will drive you crazy, and you will end up reading six minutes a day—and then seven minutes. Suddenly you will be hearing things from God and will be motivated to know Him more. And that's how love begins.

Sacrificial Love

Another aspect of love that we can measure is sacrificial love. Typically, Christians associate sacrificial love with the verse that says, "Greater love has no one than this, than to lay down one's life for his friends" (John 15:13 NKJV). We tend to think about Jesus on the cross sacrificing everything to show the depth of God's love for us. Though this is a beautiful example, sacrificial love can be less heroic, too.

Demonstrating sacrificial love can be expressed, for example, by choosing not to say the first thing that comes to your mind. Sometimes it is the most loving thing you can do to not blurt out what you are thinking. It can be holding back an email or a text message. It can mean giving someone the benefit of the doubt before you think the worst of that person.

Sacrificial love can be expressed by focusing on what you and another person agree upon rather than the hundred things upon which you disagree. It can mean picking up the phone and calling someone, telling them how much you appreciate them and saying, "I just want you to know I was thinking about you today." Sacrificial love is about doing the right thing even when the right thing can prove to be an inconvenience—that's what makes it sacrificial.

Sacrificial love does not cling to being right all the time. I tend to have this need always to be right with my kids. It's hard for me to stop and tell one of my kids, "You know, you might be right in that situation."

That's me, struggling with sacrificial love. That's me, struggling with pride. Listening to others and taking time to acknowledge them, appreciate them, and lift them up communicates how much they matter to God and how much they matter to you.

Just because we are followers of Christ doesn't mean we're perfect. It simply means we willingly commit our life and lifestyle to be more like Him. Every day we must ask ourselves if we want to call ourselves Christians that day. And if we say "yes," then our lives should reflect that of Jesus Christ.

Freedom to Move Forward

However, know that you will make mistakes of all kinds, from simple misunderstandings to terrible decisions. The blind spots we talked about previously—ignorance of our failings and weaknesses—may create mayhem. Your sinful nature may at times be overwhelmingly obvious. But God still offers freedom and a chance to recover and move forward.

Consider Peter. Peter denied Christ three times but went on to become the rock on which the church was built and a great missionary to the Gentiles.

Think of David. Although He knew his weaknesses, God had chosen David and called him "a man after His own heart" (1 Samuel 13:14 NKJV; see also Acts 13:22). He was guilty of some major sins, but he repented and asked God to search him and create a clean heart within him (Psalm 51:10).

Those who seek out their blind spots and ask God to help them recover from their mistakes reflect the heart of God. Those who chase after what it means to be a Christian will find what they're looking for. No, we aren't going to be perfect every day at following the path God has for us. But when we fall, we dust ourselves off, confess our sins, and start again.

That is the measure of a Christian.

Chapter Six Questions

Question: Are you living according to the five things God expects from us (Deuteronomy 6)? In what areas could you align your life more fully to what He desires from His people?

_____

_____

_____

_____

_____

_____

_____

_____

_____

_____

_____

_____

Question: What are three specific things you will commit to doing every day to show your love for God?

_____

_____

_____

_____

_____

_____

_____

_____

_____

_____

Question: How will you begin demonstrating sacrificial
love in everyday ways?

_____

_____

_____

_____

Action: Commit your life to becoming more like Christ and stay true to your promise every day. Write the things you're committing to do on index cards and put them where you will see them daily. Choose to love God and others, even when it's challenging or inconvenient. Don't be discouraged when you mess up. Instead, rely on God's strength and grace to help you recover and keep moving forward to become the person He wants you to be.

Chapter Six Notes

_____

_____

_____

_____

_____

_____

_____

_____

_____

_____

_____

_____

_____

_____

_____

_____

_____

_____

_____

_____

CONCLUSION

The Measure of a Legacy

I have fought a good fight, I have finished my course, I have kept the faith:

Henceforth there is laid up for me a crown of righteousness, which the Lord, the righteous judge, shall give me at that day: and not to me only, but unto all them also that love his appearing.

— 2 Timothy 4:7–8 (KJV)

It's interesting to watch track events in the Olympics. In the longer races, some runners start out far ahead of other runners, but suddenly they trail behind. Others start out slow and finish strong, or have bursts of speed along the way. But ultimately, it's about finishing a race that was well run (2 Timothy 4:7).

When your race is over, what kind of legacy will you leave? It's that legacy that will live on, being a testament to the importance of God in your life.

Now don't get me wrong. In the race that God has for you, things won't always go smoothly. You will stumble, and you will fall. *You will need help.* There will be times when you will want to give up. You will feel broken. But remember: God intends for you to finish the race, and He is going to be with you every step of the way.

Your Legacy Is Not Written in Stone

Legacies can change in an instant. A person could be a hardcore criminal his entire life but happen upon a burning vehicle with a family trapped inside, rescue that family, and in one moment change his legacy. He is no longer a criminal, but a hero. Was it a criminal saved by a family? Or was it a family saved by a criminal?

Plenty of people live their lives doing everything right. They have been kind, compassionate, and caring. They have done all the right things. Then they might decide to have a one-night stand or to rob a bank. In that moment of weakness, their legacy will be changed.

We saw earlier how, in one moment in AD 33, a criminal's legacy changed forever. Jesus was hanging on the cross with a criminal to His left and another to His right. One said to Jesus, "Lord, remember me when You come into Your kingdom" (Luke 23:42 NKJV). Jesus responded, "Assuredly, I say to you, today you will be with Me in Paradise" (Luke 23:43 NKJV). This criminal's legacy changed in a moment from an enemy of God to God's child. We know nothing about this man's past, but we know everything about his future.

You may have chosen selfishness yesterday, but you can still choose generosity and joy today. You may have relied on your own strength in the past, but you can rely on God today.

The race is not over. There is still time to make a change and fully live up to the measure of a Christian.

Finding Strength

We've talked about going all in with God and trusting Him to come through. We've talked about having joy and generosity even when we don't feel like it. We've looked at taking the high road and being the better person when our sinful nature is telling us otherwise. We've covered knowing our true value and living that out. And we've discussed what it means to be a blessing to other people.

But more than anything, the core component of being a Christian is to love God and love others.

While we can have an idea of how we're doing in each of these areas, the fact of the matter is that it's not an easy process! Each and every day is a struggle, and I'll admit sometimes I fall off the path completely. Some days I don't measure up to half of what a Christian should be.

On our own strength, we're helpless. But we're not meant to do this on our own.

God loves you and wants you to cross that finish line and leave the most incredible legacy. However, you must be willing to let Him come alongside you and put His arm around you so you can lean into His shoulder. God sees your brokenness. He longs to comfort you and to carry you along in the race toward the finish line.

God will push away those who attempt to stop you, or

who tell you that it's too late or you don't have what it takes to finish. However, you must be willing to trust Him with all your heart, with all your soul, and with all your strength.

Who you were yesterday doesn't have to be who you are today. The metamorphosis is sometimes difficult, but that's why God is with you. And He is saying the same thing He has always said.

Trust Me.

Notes

1. *Braveheart*. Directed by Mel Gibson. Paramount Pictures, 1995.
2. CBS Boston. "55 Drive-Thru Customers Part of 'Pay It Forward' Chain at Amesbury Donut Shop." *CBS Local*. CBS Broadcasting Inc. July 13, 2013. http://boston.cbslocal.com/2013/07/13/55-drive-thru-customers-part-of-pay-it-forward-chain-at-amesbury-donut-shop.
3. Covey, Stephen. *Seven Habits of Highly Effective People*. Free Press, 1989.
4. Maxwell, John C. *Winning with People: Discover the People Principles That Work for You Every Time*. Thomas Nelson, 2007, 224–225.
5. *Spider-Man*. Directed by Sam Raimi. Columbia, Pictures, 2002.
6. Make-A-Wish America. "Landry Builds the Ultimate Treehouse with Make-A-Wish Philadelphia." *YouTube*. July 21, 2016. https://www.youtube.com/watch?v=HipR6qrcw1

g.
7. "2618. chesed." *Strong's Exhaustive Concordance*. In *Bible Hub*. Bible Hub, Inc. biblehub.com/str/hebrew/2618.htm.

About Tim May

I entered the ministry because I was looking for sustainable joy and purpose. I discovered that helping people learn how to live with *passion* and *clarity* as the best expression of a *beloved* child of God is where I would find that joy and purpose.

My experience as a Navy chaplain and a United Methodist pastor has revealed to me that there are a lot of amazing people in the world who want to do remarkable things. They imagine the impossible, but when it comes to getting out of the boat, they remain stuck in their seat.

This book is one of my attempts to get out of the boat. I wrote this book believing that God might use my writing to influence and impact hundreds of people.

I was not always a Christian. In fact, I consider myself a recovered atheist. I grew up in a military family, specifically a Navy family. Life was challenging, and those challenges often created a space for me to question everything about life, including the existence of God. The answers I received were never satisfying, especially my questions about God, suffering, and bad things happening to good people. My questions created more doubt and uncertainty in my already chaotic and strange world.

At the age of 20, I battled with deep sadness, loneliness, and a significant identity crisis (I know, who suffers from an identity crisis at 20?). I decided to take the advice of a Christian and go and talk to a military chaplain.

My encounter with the chaplain was my first experience with a guide (coach). He shared a lot of things that made sense to me and revealed some of my faulty thinking in a way that did not make me feel stupid or naïve. He created a space that allowed me to be open and honest with my thoughts and feelings. That encounter has served as a foundation for the ways I attempt to guide others through my writing, preaching, teaching, and coaching.

The people for whom I want to serve as a guide, the people I write for, are people who want to be a light of hope, joy, and inspiration for others. They want to commit their lives to helping others experience the power of having a breakthrough. They want to experience the joy that comes in assisting others with doing what seems impossible.

My life is a blessed life. I am married to my beautiful college sweetheart, and together we have three amazing children, ages 13, 8, and 7.

I am a Commander in the Navy Reserves, and I pastor a magnificent church in Fort Pierce, Florida. I love to exercise, play golf, and watch *Big Bang Theory*, *Marvel's Agents of S.H.I.E.L.D*, and all the Marvel movies. I am also a Pittsburgh Steelers fan. At the end of the day, I am just an ordinary husband, father, and Christian, who is trying to inspire as many people as possible to live as *beloved* children of God.

About Sermon To Book

SermonToBook.com began with a simple belief: that sermons should be touching lives, *not* collecting dust. That's why we turn sermons into high-quality books that are accessible to people all over the globe.

Turning your sermon series into a book exposes more people to God's Word, better equips you for counseling, accelerates future sermon prep, adds credibility to your ministry, and even helps make ends meet during tight times.

John 21:25 tells us that the world itself couldn't contain the books that would be written about the work of Jesus Christ. Our mission is to try anyway. Because in heaven, there will no longer be a need for sermons or books. Our time is now.

If God so leads you, we'd love to work with you on your sermon or sermon series.

Visit www.sermontobook.com to learn more.

Made in the USA
Columbia, SC
26 August 2018